How Good is your Limit Hold'em?

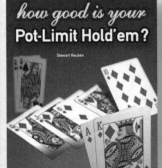
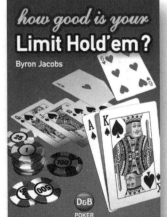

how good is your Limit Hold'em?

Byron Jacobs with **Jim Brier**

D&B PUBLISHING
www.dandbpublishing.com

First published in 2005 by D & B Publishing, PO Box 18,
Hassocks, West Sussex BN6 9WR

British Library Cataloguing-in-Publication Data
A catalogue record for this book is available from the British Library.

ISBN 1-904468-15-2

All sales enquiries should be directed to:
D & B Publishing, PO Box 18, Hassocks, West Sussex BN6 9WR, UK
Tel: (+44) 1273 834680; Fax: (+44) 1273 831629
e-mail: info@dandbpublishing.com,
Website: www.dandbpublishing.com

Cover design by Horatio Monteverde
Production by Navigator Guides
Printed and bound in the US by Versa Press

Contents

♣ — ♥ — ♦ — ♠ — ♣ — ♥ — ♦ — ♠

Hands   11,12

Introduction

♣ — ♥ — ♦ — ♠ — ♣ — ♥ — ♦ — ♠

There are many very good books on limit hold'em. Some are aimed at complete beginners, whereas others cater for experienced players who want to play at a more advanced level. This book is certainly not a book for beginners. It is aimed at players who have a reasonable understanding of the game of limit hold'em, and already have some experience of either online or live play. Specifically, it is about trying to move up from the low-limit games ($3-$6 and $5-$10) in order to compete successfully at the middle limits ($10-$20, $15-$30 and $20-$40).

I have been playing online poker for around three years, and I found it particularly difficult to make this move up in limits. Once I had learned the game I found that, after a few months, I could survive reasonably well at the low limit level. I possessed decent pre-flop standards and could play competently beyond the flop, but no more. This modest ability was sufficient to compete as a small favourite in the $3-$6 and $5-$10 games.

However, when I tried to move up to the middle-limit games, I felt way out of my depth. In fact, due to a fortunate run of cards, my initial forays at this level were quite successful. However, things quickly turned against me, and I soon realised that I needed to understand the game much better to compete successfully beyond the low limits.

There are a number of hold'em books that address the problems that arise when playing at the middle limits. Such books often give excellent advice on dealing with specific technical situations. However, they often make the assumption that all of your opponents are of identical skill or all play exactly the same game. Some of them presume that your opponents are all solid and actually play rather well, whereas others appear to take the view that your opposition has just arrived from the local fish shop.

The reality of playing at the middle limits is actually quite different. You meet all kinds of players at these levels. As this is the highest limit on many online sites, you naturally will run into many very decent players in these games. However, you will also find many, many other types of player: solid, unimaginative plodders; decent players who call down too much; weak players; maniacs; very weak players; very weak players who are also maniacs; pre-flop maniacs who actually play sensibly post-flop; players who are addicted to the semi-bluff raise; untutored naturals who play strange cards but play them rather well; players for whom the only possible explanation for their play is that they are experiencing an altered state of consciousness, etc. The list is endless.

To be successful at the middle limits, it is not enough just to play a solid technical game. You must learn to identify the weak opponents at the table, and recognise the features of their play that make them weak. You then need to understand and utilise specific strategies to cope with their play and get their money.

However, the dynamics of the game complicate this further. You will rarely find yourself nicely positioned, playing a good hand, heads-up against a known weak and timid player. A more familiar scenario is that you find yourself in a pot with perhaps two other players, one of whom you may know to be a maniac, but the other may be a complete unknown, or perhaps you are aware that they are actually a very good player. If you can successfully handle the complex dynamics of such pots, then you will be a winning player at the middle limits.

These dynamics are what this book is about. In nearly all cases I will identify features of the playing style of your opponents in the hands. This may be a brief summary or it may be more detailed. Occasionally I will present you with an opponent about whom you know nothing. You must bear in mind what is known about your opponents when making the decisions on the hands. This is crucial. It is quite common for there to be a situation where it is correct to fold against one opponent and raise against another.

I have chosen to present the material in the form of complete hands and to flesh these out with hypothetical situations. Many other books are split into chapters on pre-flop play, flop play, turn play etc. There is nothing wrong with this approach, but I think that it is instructive to follow a hand through from beginning to end. After all, that's how we play poker. We don't spend one evening just playing pre-flop and the next just the river.

All the hands in this book are taken from online play. Many of them actually occurred more or less as given, but I have occasionally adapted some of the features to make a point. I have given the players in this book names which are emphatically *not* the handles of the players who were involved in the pots. Many other books refer to players simply by their actions, but I find this approach a little impersonal. It also becomes rather unwieldy when the author is reduced to writing something inelegant like: 'The pre-flop raiser bets out and the pre-flop re-raiser now raises...'

I will offer the standard disclaimer that the names I have chosen are fictitious and that any resemblance to players living, dead or temporarily bankrupt, is purely coincidental. However, there are hundreds of thousands of online players, and it is inevitable that some of the names I have chosen here will duplicate actual player's handles. I emphasise – this is purely coincidental.

Finally, I would like to thank Jim Brier, who is well known to serious hold'em players as the author (with Bob Ciaffone) of *Middle Limit Holdem*, and also as columnist for the *Card Player* magazine. Jim kindly agreed to act as 'consultant' on the book, and made many helpful suggestions with the explanations offered in the 'Answers and Analysis' sections of the book. I would also like to thank Andrew Kinsman, who did his usual fine editing job.

I am very happy to receive feedback on the material here and can be contacted at byronajacobs@aol.com.

Byron Jacobs
Brighton
April 2005

Online Play

♣ – ♥ – ♦ – ♠ – ♣ – ♥ – ♦ – ♠

Online Playing Styles

One key feature of online play is the ability to download and save previous hands. These can then be imported into a database package (the leaders here are Poker Tracker and PokerStat) and analysed at leisure. Both of these packages do an excellent job of extracting all kinds of information about the way you play, and help you to discover the strengths and weaknesses of your game. Perhaps even more importantly, they allow you to build profiles of your regular opponents. Developing and analysing these is crucial to your potential success as an online player, especially beyond the low limits.

In this book I have therefore placed great emphasis on providing information about how your opponents play: whether they are strong or weak, loose or tight, aggressive or passive. There are many difficult decisions in a poker game, and knowledge of your opponents often determines how you should act. Poker is a highly situational game, and frequently there are no purely right or wrong answers. In one scenario it may very well be best to raise against one particular player and yet to fold against another.

In the hands that follow I will often give indications about the playing style of your opponents, and you should bear these in mind before making your decisions. The three major ways to define a player's style are as follows: loose or tight, aggressive or passive, strong or weak. I would now like to discuss each of these in turn.

Loose or Tight

One of the key decisions – possibly *the* most important decision – in a hold'em game is whether you will get involved in the pot or not. The frequency with which you do this defines whether you are loose or tight. Loose players enter the pot too often, whereas tight players are more selective about which starting hands they will play.

With the benefit of the statistics packages that are available, it is a straightforward matter to discern who is loose and who is tight. These packages will typically offer a statistic such as the percentage of times that a player voluntarily puts money in the pot pre-flop. When you have enough data on a player, this is a key statistic in determining whether you want them in your game or not. In a full ring game, anyone who is entering more than 35% of pots is playing too loose. Such players can have some remarkable winning sessions, but they cannot get the money in the long run. The gods of probability will simply not allow it. These are the players you want in your game. Even playing 30% of pots is on the loose side, and good, tight players will play around 20-25% of their hands. Anyone who plays less than 20% of their hands is super-tight. Such players are not much fun to have in the game, since they will not throw their money at you. However, if you have to play with them, then it is good to sit near them. In general, they tend not to defend their blinds sufficiently, and they are also less inclined to attack yours.

There is a certain type of tight player who *is* good to have in the game. This is the tight player who cannot release his hands. He waits so long to get involved in pots that he cannot bear to let go of his hand. If he has a bare A-K he will stubbornly call all the way to the river, even though someone is more or less telling him that they have at least a pair. If he has 9-9 and the flop is A-Q-T, he just calls down, presumably hoping that his opponent is pumping away with precisely a pair of 8s. Weak players often fail to consider what cards their opponents can be holding; players like this don't even consider what cards are on the board.

Aggressive or Passive

The frequency with which a player bets or raises – as opposed to checking or calling – defines whether they are aggressive or passive. Successful poker players are nearly always aggressive – they take the initiative in pots with bets and raises. Checking and calling – playing follow my leader – is rarely a profitable strategy. Nevertheless, many players do play like this.

This is, again, an area where the stats packages can be very useful. If you look at a player's statistics, you can generally develop a feel as to what their style of play is in this respect. However, a word of warning is necessary here. There are many players who are very aggressive pre-flop, but then crawl back into their shell when the flop comes (especially on the turn when the bet size doubles). Poker Tracker, for example, offers an 'aggression index' – a helpful tool which offers an overall measure of a player's aggression throughout the hand. However, this must be used with care as it is an aggregate over all four betting rounds.

Naturally, you want to be in games with the passive players, who spend most of their poker careers in check-call mode. Limit poker is all about extracting that extra bet on your winning hands, and saving a bet when you are dealt a pay-off hand. Passive players are mightily helpful in this respect: they fail to push hard enough on their good hands, and then often pay you off when you have the goods.

Although aggressive players are more problematic, if you identify that you are up against someone who fits this description, then you can modify your play accordingly. If you are heads-up with a big hand and out of position, you can be more confident about trying for a check-raise. Alternatively, if you have position, you can more confidently wait for the turn to pull the trigger, rather than announcing strength on the flop.

Aggressive players tend to bluff and semi-bluff more, and this can be picked up by considering the statistic which states how often a player wins in a showdown. A solid winning player generally has a showdown win rate in the high 50s, say 58%. Any solid winning player with a lower showdown win rate is probably also highly aggressive. They take down more pots pre-river with aggressive play, but this is counter-balanced by the fact that they often get found out on the river by a stubborn opponent. The tell-tale sign on the balance sheet of this style of play is the lower than average showdown win rate.

I once found myself heads-up in a $15-$30 game with a player I knew to be aggressive. Although I had faced him often, it had not been for a while and, at the time, I didn't have a particularly good feel for his play. I was holding 10-10 and the flop came with three rags. He bet, I raised and he three-bet. I just called, although capping may well have been a better play. The turn was a king, which wasn't a good card for me, but now he suddenly checked. I bet fairly quickly and he fired back with a raise. I now really wasn't sure what to do, but this check-raise is a strong play and my inclination was to muck my hand. It would cost a further $60 dollars to see it through and, as there were no obvious drawing possibilities, I could very easily be playing just two outs. However, I quickly flicked over to Poker Tracker, keyed in his name and noticed that his showdown win rate was only 49%, despite the fact that he was a pretty decent winner over more than 2,000 hands. Therefore I decided to call him down.

This turned out to be a classic case of the operation being a success, but the patient dying. The river was a queen and he took the pot with Q-J!

Strong or Weak

Now that we have discussed loose and tight, aggressive and passive, we need to understand what makes a strong player. Strong players invariably play in a tight-aggressive manner. Weak players tend to play in a loose-passive manner. Of course there are variations; there are some quite decent players who play in a loose-aggressive manner, and also those who play tight-passive.

Naturally, it is better to try and play your hands against weak players. Weak players come in many different forms but, in general, they will usually be loose, they will tend not to bet their good hands hard enough, and they will call you down with insufficient values. They will also draw to long shots that are not justified by pot odds considerations. However, if you play your poker at the middle limits and higher, it will not always be possible to find games exclusively populated by weak players. Therefore you will inevitably have to tangle with strong players, and you will have to navigate these dangerous waters competently if you are to be successful.

It is not all bad news to find yourself in pots with good players. There are often ways to take pots off good players that are simply not available against weaker ones. The most obvious is the bluff or semi-bluff. Weak players, in general, are unwilling to fold their hands, so trying to push them out of pots is hard work. Better players want to save bets, and are more willing to dump hands that they suspect are beaten. Better players are also more likely to make bluff and semi-bluff plays themselves. Suppose that someone gives you a lot of heat (maybe raising you on the turn), when you have a reasonable, but not overwhelming, holding. You should be more inclined to call down against a good player than a 'fish'. The good player may well be trying to barge you out of the pot, whereas the weak player is usually just betting his monster hand.

However, it is not advisable to get too fancy against good players. The key thing here is to pick your moments. Good players are successful because they understand what is going on at the table and what other players are thinking. They know all about semi-bluff raises, and if you are free and easy with such plays you will quickly find that they are not folding against you, but three-betting. You may well then end up making a mess of a reasonable drawing opportunity by paying way over the odds for your draw.

MrNormal

Many of the hands that follow will feature players about whom you know nothing. You will not have come across them before, and they have probably only recently sat down in the game, so they are more or less a completely unknown quantity. We will assume, not always correctly, that such players are of a competent standard without being world beaters. They may just have moved up from a lower limit, and thus may well be a little anxious at this 'new' level.

I would now like to offer a profile of a typical 'normal' player who competes at the $10-$20 to $20-$40 level. When you come across such a 'normal' player in the hands, you can assume that he conforms broadly to the following profile.

Pre-flop he will be reasonably sound but a little loose, playing a few more hands than is strictly justified. His opening standards when he is first to speak will probably be quite good, but the slightly loose nature of his pre-flop play will manifest itself in unjustified limps and calls of raises. The following plays are typical of MrNormal:

1) The UTG limps. It is folded round to MrNormal in middle position, who calls with hands such as 8♣-7♣, 4♣-4♠, J♦-T♥, A♥-3♥. None of these calls are justified, as only one player is in the pot, and there are many players to come who may raise. A likely scenario is that MrNormal will end up paying a double bet to contest a pot three-handed, where he doesn't have good odds for his drawing hand.

2) A middle player open-raises and another middle player calls. It is folded round to MrNormal on the button, who now calls with K♠-T♠, 6♥-6♣, A♠-T♥. Again, none of these calls are justified.

MrNormal will probably also be slightly too keen to contest the pot for one more bet, from the big blind. Many players cannot resist coming along from the big blind for just one bet as the pot odds look so attractive. For example, in a $20-$40 game an early player raises and is called by the button and the small blind. Our hero is sitting in the big blind with some piece of junk like 8♣-5♣ or K♠-8♥. He can see $140 in the pot and 7-to-1 pot odds. He can also assume that, whatever the flop, if the small blind checks and he checks too, there is quite likely to be at least a bet and a call by the time the action gets back to him. His pot odds could be up to 8-to-1 or 9-to-1. Surely, he thinks, it is worth the $20 just to see the flop? He might hit two pair, or trips, or a straight or a flush draw. It's *only* $20 dollars... Calls such as these are a foolproof strategy for allowing your funds to dribble away, but many players do make them.

Post-flop MrNormal again plays reasonably sensibly, but there are typically three areas to note in his game.

1) He calls too much. After the flop in limit hold'em you should be doing a

fair amount of betting and raising, a lot of folding, and not much calling. However, MrNormal calls too much. He calls when he should be raising to protect his hand, and he calls when his hand should be hitting the muck. He *is* capable of mucking hands but, on the whole, he goes to the river rather more often than he should.

2) He loves to check-raise his good hands. Check-raising is a strong play that is an important tool in the arsenal of any good player, but MrNormal overdoes it. If he calls pre-flop and then lands a monster he will call on the flop, wait for the turn and then – ding! – in comes the check-raise. This is certainly not a bad way to play, but good players will pick up on this easily, and it will enable them to get away from trap hands without paying off. Stronger players will vary their play more with their good hands and be harder to read.

3) The first two points are areas of weakness in MrNormal's game. However, there is a hold'em tactic which he uses rather well – the semi-bluff. This is one of the strengths in MrNormal's game. Semi-bluffing is often a powerful play, and it is well documented in hold'em literature. MrNormal has a good handle on the semi-bluff and can often use it effectively. This is a particular nuisance for you – the good (I hope!) hold'em player. Being a good player you hate to pay off. As such you recognise that you have to be prepared to muck some quite decent hands, when the evidence suggests they are beaten and the odds are not there to chase. This saves crucial bets. However, MrNormal's competence with the semi-bluff creates problems and – occasionally – obliges you to call down with hands that you suspect are beaten.

How to use this Book

♣ — ♥ — ♦ — ♠ — ♣ — ♥ — ♦ — ♠

Structure and Terminology

The hands in this book are all taken from online $15-$30 and $20-$40 games. Some are more or less exactly as they happened, some have been adapted, and one or two have been invented in order to make a point. The following notes apply to all the hands:

In the $20-$40 games, the small blind is $10 and the big blind is $20.

In the $15-$30 games, the small blind is $10 and the big blind is $15.

Each round of betting consists of a bet and three possible raises. The betting unit is the size of the big blind pre-flop and on the flop, and then doubles for the turn and river betting. As is standard in online games, the betting is capped by the third raise, even if the pot is heads-up at that stage. Thus in a $20-$40 game the maximum that each player can bet on any one round pre-flop and on the flop is $80, and on the turn and river it is $160.

The 'UTG' is the under-the-gun player, sitting directly on the left hand side of the big blind. This player is first to speak after the pre-flop cards are dealt. The button is the dealer and is last to speak on all post-flop rounds. The cut-off is the player directly to the right of the button. In a full ring game of ten players, I have used early position to refer to the UTG player and the next two positions; middle position comprises the next three players, whereas late position refers to the cut-off and the button. The other two players in the hand are the small blind and the big blind.

For simplicity, I have exclusively used the pronoun 'he' throughout the text to refer to the players.

You can assume that players fold their hands unless otherwise indicated. To keep things simple, no rake is deducted from the pot totals, although this would typically be $2-$3 per deal.

If you want to read this book purely for entertainment, and in the hope of finding some useful advice along the way, then please go ahead. However, if you are seriously interested in evaluating and improving your hold'em play, then I strongly suggest that you play through the hands and decide what you would do in each particular situation.

The best way to do this is to work your way through all of the questions for each hand before checking any of the answers. You should not assume that the player of the hand, often myself, made the optimal choice. In this way you will come to each decision 'cold', and will avoid receiving any hint which will help you to answer the remaining questions in the hand. Thus, as far as possible, the play will follow that of a 'live' hand. The analysis of each hand appears at its conclusion.

Scoring System

The total points available for each hand is 100. However, some of the decisions on the hand are much more straightforward than others. Indeed, there is often a key moment where making the right decision is crucial. Therefore, although many of the questions score ten points for a correct answer, there is some variation around this, with some scoring only five points and others as much as 30. This is not indicated in the question itself, so you will not know whether you are sweating over a five-point or 30-point problem.

Experienced poker players may be somewhat sceptical of the very concept of a poker puzzle book. There are, they will argue, no right or wrong answers about certain situations. The game revolves around elements such as 'feel' and 'psychology', and there is no way to dilute such amorphous concepts into simple rights and wrongs. This may well be true of live no-limit poker, and situations can arise in such games for which no amount of technical knowledge can prepare you. However, playing online limit poker is a very different proposition, since there is much greater opportunity to make technically accurate plays that will take down the money in the long run. This is especially true if you can keep data on your regular opponents and form accurate profiles of them.

What Limit Hold'em is all about

Poker is often perceived by the general public as a highly flamboyant game, in which high rollers make outrageous bluffs and browbeat the opposition into submission by sheer force of personality. This perception, in the main fuelled by the depiction of poker in films, is way off the mark. Admittedly no-limit poker, especially in the later stages of tournaments, can sometimes be like that, but limit poker is an altogether different beast.

Limit hold'em is about grinding away and exploiting small edges. If you play at the middle limits and higher – the level of play at which the hands in this book are aimed – then the majority of your opponents are going to be at the very least moderately competent, and some will be a whole lot better than that. To be successful, you will need to play well enough to maintain a small edge, and to be able to nurse that small edge over a great number of hands and sessions.

In the long run, everyone receives basically the same cards at hold'em. We are all dealt big hands that win, big hands that lose, modest hands that win and modest hands that lose. If you continuously get dealt the pay-off hands during a session then, even if you are the very best limit hold'em player in the world, you are still going to lose money. It is very difficult to turn losing hands into winning ones in limit play (except perhaps at heads-up and short-handed games). Most of the time, a bet made in the later stages of the hand is going to offer the opposition odds of maybe 8-to-1 or 9-to-1 to call. Players are not going to readily dump their hands when the odds are this good.

The difference between the good player and the merely competent player, is that the good player will earn slightly more with the winning hands and lose slightly less with the losing hands. Let's say that a player has a horrible session of 300 hands at $20-$40 where almost nothing goes right. The good player might lose $1,200; the weaker player might lose a little more, say $1,360. Thus the good player has 'won' $160. It usually takes around four hours to play 300 hands online. Thus, despite ending well down on the session, the good player has 'won' $40, or one big bet, per hour. This equates to just four good folds in a four-hour session.

This will be very much the emphasis of the hands here. Often you will have a hand that is, unfortunately, just going to lose money. The skill comes from ensuring that rather than dropping $120 with the hand, you see the danger and only lose $90. Despite the fact that you have just lost money, your good play means that the hand has been a success. When a weaker player gets the same hand, he or she will lose $120, or maybe more – and you may well be the beneficiary.

When you are competing for a pot, a question you should constantly ask yourself is: how can I best play this hand to maximise my potential profit, and also to minimise the loss if it goes against me? Hopefully this book will help you to arrive at the correct decisions to pursue these joint strategies.

Hand 1

Bizarre Bunch

INTRODUCTION

This is a seven-player $20-$40 game. You are in the big blind with
A♣-10♣. Jonny has just joined the game and is in the cut-off. He posts
$20. You have come across him before. He is a competent player but nothing special, and plays a quiet solid game. He is fairly timid and rather
loose pre-flop, and you don't expect fireworks from him. The UTG is Bizarre – a strange player who makes odd plays, typically playing his good
hands too passively and his mediocre hands too aggressively. He too is
rather loose pre-flop.

THE PLAY

Pre-flop

Bizarre opens with a raise.

Hypothetical Play

It is folded around to Jonny who now three-bets (note that this is 'only'
$40 for him as he has posted a late blind). The button and small blind
fold. There is $130 in the pot and it is $40 to you.

Question 1. Do you (a) fold (b) call (c) raise?

| (a) ☐ | (b) ☐ | (c) ☐ | Points: .... |

Actual Play

It is folded round to Jonny who calls. The button and small blind fold.
There is $110 in the pot and it is $20 to you.

Question 2. Do you (a) fold (b) call (c) raise?

(a) ☐	(b) ☐	(c) ☐	Points: ....

You call.

Flop

The flop comes down 10♥-8♥-6♦. You hold A♣-10♣.

There is $130 in the pot and it is $20 to bet.

Question 3. Do you (a) check, planning to call (b) check, planning a check-raise (c) bet?

(a) ☐	(b) ☐	(c) ☐	Points: ....

You bet and Bizarre raises. Jonny thinks for a moment and then calls the two bets cold. There is $230 in the pot and it is $20 to you.

Question 4. Do you (a) fold (b) call (c) raise?

(a) ☐	(b) ☐	(c) ☐	Points: ....

You call.

Turn

The turn is 10♥-8♥-6♦-6♠. You hold A♣-10♣. There is $250 in the pot and it is $40 to bet.

Question 5. Do you (a) check, planning to call (b) check, planning a check-raise (c) bet?

(a) ☐	(b) ☐	(c) ☐	Points: ....

You bet.

Hypothetical Play 1

Bizarre now calls and Jonny raises. There is $410 in the pot and it is $40 to you.

Question 6. Do you (a) fold (b) call (c) raise?

(a) ☐	(b) ☐	(c) ☐	Points: ....

Hypothetical Play 2

Bizarre now raises. Jonny thinks for a while and calls. There is $450 in the pot and it is $40 to you.

Question 7. Do you (a) fold (b) call (c) raise?

(a) ☐	(b) ☐	(c) ☐		Points: ....

Actual Play

Bizarre calls, as does Jonny.

River

Hypothetical River

The river is 10♥-8♥-6♦-6♠-3♣. You hold A♣-10♣.

There is $370 in the pot and it is $40 to bet.

Question 8. Do you (a) check (b) bet?

(a) ☐	(b) ☐	Points: ....

Actual River

The river is 10♥-8♥-6♦-6♠-K♣. You hold A♣-10♣.

There is $370 in the pot and it is $40 to bet.

Question 9. Do you (a) check (b) bet?

(a) ☐	(b) ☐	Points: .... **Total:** ....

You bet, Bizarre folds and Jonny calls. You take the pot with a pair of 10s with an ace kicker. The hand history shows that Jonny held 10♦-9♦.

♣ − ♥ − ♦ − ♠ − ♣ − ♥ − ♦ − ♠

SCORECHART

100	Excellent. Good aggressive play.
90-99	Very good. You could not have missed much here.
80-89	Good. Maybe you need to be more aggressive with your strong hands.
70-79	You probably need to take the initiative more.
60-69	This shows a definite reluctance to bet your hands for value.
below 60	Poor.

♣ — ♥ — ♦ — ♠ — ♣ — ♥ — ♦ — ♠

ANSWERS AND ANALYSIS

Holding: A♣-10♣.

Question 1. (a) 10 (b) 3 (c) 0

Jonny is marked out as a solid player, and it is best to fold as your hand is most likely dominated by his. It is a shame not to be able to play your hand, as it would certainly have been good for one bet. However, two small bets are too much to pay, out of position with a solid player announcing a big hand.

You might argue that since Jonny had already posted a late blind, he was coming in cheaply and thus his three-bet might be made on light values, especially if he knows that Bizarre is loose. However, this doesn't really hold water. Jonny is solid and – with any sort of respectable holding – he had an easy call for one bet. However, he has chosen to escalate the pot; he must therefore have something pretty decent.

Question 2. (a) 0 (b) 5 (c) 2

Re-raising is too frisky as you are out of position with an unpredictable player immediately to your right. There is nothing wrong with a simple call.

Flop: 10♥-8♥-6♦. You hold A♣-10♣.

Question 3. (a) 0 (b) 10 (c) 15

The board is quite coordinated, and there are many drawing possibilities. It would be criminal to give a free card here and, for that reason alone, it is almost mandatory to bet. If you check, you cannot be sure that Bizarre will bet. Even if he does bet, Jonny calls and you then check-raise, you are not going to get anybody out.

Question 4. (a) 0 (b) 15 (c) 8

You have top pair, top kicker so folding, for the moment, is out of the question. You may well be winning, but this is probably not the moment to raise. Bizarre's raise could be made on a wide range of hands and Jonny also has something decent. Rather than escalating the pot now I prefer to see the turn card before deciding what to do next. If something horrible like the 7♥ comes then you can bow out gracefully.

Turn: 10♥-8♥-6♦-6♠. You hold A♣-10♣.

Question 5. (a) 5 (b) 0 (c) 15

This is a very good time to bet as the 6♠ has probably not helped anyone. At least one of your opponents holds a drawing hand and both may do so. If you check now there is again a great danger that you will give a free card. You have enough of a hand to call, so try to take the initiative with a bet.

Question 6. (a) 15 (b) 2 (c) 0

Jonny has sprung to life and it is time to give up. Both you and Bizarre have shown strength in this hand and yet Jonny, marked as a solid player, is raising you both. At the very least he has a 6 in his hand and he may be much stronger. You cannot possibly have enough outs to justify continuing in the hand.

Question 7. (a) 7 (b) 10 (c) 0

You are probably losing, but you have several advantages here over the scenario from Question 6.

a) Your pot odds are slightly better.

b) The raise came from a known unpredictable player rather than a solid one.

c) You can be fairly sure you are beating Jonny, as it looks like he has a drawing hand. You could, of course, be in big trouble against Bizarre, but it is also possible that he just has a very good drawing hand. Note that if he has an overpair (not aces) – which is possible as he open-raised – then you could have as many as five outs (three aces and two 10s), and thus have pot odds.

Even so, folding is not terrible as the hand will probably cost $80 to see out, and you can very easily be outdrawn.

River: 10♥-8♥-6♦-6♠-K♣. You hold A♣-10♣.

Question 8. (a) 0 (b) 5

You bet the turn and didn't get raised. You are almost certainly winning. Bet the river and pick up some crying calls.

Question 9. (a) 2 (b) 10

It is most unlikely that the king has helped anyone. It is crucial to pick up extra bets in hold'em. The pot is large and you will get calls here, even from quite weak hands.

♣ — ♥ — ♦ — ♠ — ♣ — ♥ — ♦ — ♠

TIP: When you get raised on the flop but the turn card appears to be harmless, it is often best to lead out again. This avoids giving a potential free card and helps you to judge where you stand in the hand.

Hand 2

Caught in the Headlights

♣ — ♥ — ♦ — ♠ — ♣ — ♥ — ♦ — ♠

INTRODUCTION

This is a ten-player $15-$30 game. You are in middle position with
A♠-K♠. The cut-off is Madness, a loose and rather aggressive player. The
big blind is TheRabbit. TheRabbit is a delightful player to have in the
game – loose, passive and utterly transparent. He is also rather timid –
not the kind of player to make pressure plays.

THE PLAY

Pre-flop

It is passed around to you. There is $25 in the pot and it is $15 to call.

Question 1. Do you: (a) fold (b) call (c) raise?

(a) ☐	(b) ☐	(c) ☐	Points: ....

You raise.

Hypothetical Play

Madness calls and TheRabbit now raises. There is $115 in the pot and it
is $15 to you.

Question 2. Do you (a) fold (b) call (c) raise?

(a) ☐	(b) ☐	(c) ☐	Points: ....

Actual Play

Madness calls, as does TheRabbit.

Flop

The flop is Q♠-10♣-4♣. You hold A♠-K♠.

TheRabbit checks. There is $100 in the pot and it is $15 to bet.

Question 3. Do you (a) check (b) bet?

(a) ☐	(b) ☐		Points: ....

You bet.

Hypothetical Play

Madness raises and TheRabbit three-bets. There is $190 in the pot and it is $30 to you.

Question 4. Do you: (a) fold (b) call (c) raise?

(a) ☐	(b) ☐	(c) ☐	Points: ....

Actual Play

Madness folds and TheRabbit now check-raises you. There is $145 in the pot and it is $15 to you.

Question 5. Do you: (a) fold (b) call (c) raise?

(a) ☐	(b) ☐	(c) ☐	Points: ....

You raise.

Hypothetical Play

TheRabbit now caps and you call. The turn brings Q♠-10♣-4♣-2♥ and TheRabbit bets out. There is $250 in the pot and it is $30 to you.

Question 6. Do you: (a) fold (b) call (c) raise?

(a) ☐	(b) ☐	(c) ☐	Points: ....

Actual Play

TheRabbit calls.

Turn

Hypothetical Turn

The turn is Q♠-10♣-4♣-10♠. You hold A♠-K♠.

TheRabbit checks. There is $190 in the pot and it is $30 to bet.

Question 7. Do you (a) check (b) bet?

(a) ☐ (b) ☐	Points: ....

Actual Turn

The turn is Q♠-10♣-4♣-8♥. You hold A♠-K♠. TheRabbit checks. There is $190 in the pot and it is $30 to bet.

Question 8. Do you (a) check (b) bet?

(a) ☐ (b) ☐	Points: ....

You check.

River

The river is Q♠-10♣-4♣-8♥-J♣. You hold A♠-K♠.

TheRabbit now bets. There is $220 in the pot and it is $30 to you.

Question 9. Do you: (a) fold (b) call (c) raise?

(a) ☐ (b) ☐ (c) ☐	Points: ....

You raise and TheRabbit calls. Your straight takes the pot from TheRabbit's two pair with Q♦-J♠.

Question 10. The river card, 8♥, put four to a straight on board. Therefore, did TheRabbit make a mistake by betting his two pair on the river: (a) yes (b) no?

(a) ☐ (b) ☐	Points: ....
	Total: ....

♣ — ♥ — ♦ — ♠ — ♣ — ♥ — ♦ — ♠

SCORECHART

100   Excellent. You handled your overcards very well.

90-99   Very good.

80-89   Good. You probably need to think harder about when to push with your overcards and when to back off.

70-79   Average.

60-69   Never mind. Handling overcards is tricky.

below 60   Poor.

♣ – ♥ – ♦ – ♠ – ♣ – ♥ – ♦ – ♠

ANSWERS AND ANALYSIS

Holding: A♠-K♠.

Question 1. (a) 0 (b) 1 (c) 5

Calling (and hoping to re-raise) is possible with the absolute premium hands such as A-A and K-K. However, with A-K suited you are really hoping to get heads-up or in a three-way pot where your hand has some chance to win even if it doesn't improve. Limping is more justifiable with weaker hands such as Q-J suited and K-J suited.

Question 2. (a) 0 (b) 5 (c) 4

TheRabbit's three-bet from the big blind suggests a very strong holding. You have position over him and seeing the flop for just one more small bet is preferable to getting frisky with a raise. Nevertheless, you have a very big hand and raising is not really a mistake.

Flop: Q♠-10♣-4♣. You hold A♠-K♠.

Question 3. (a) 2 (b) 10

Checking might get you a free card, but it also tells the world that you don't have a great deal. Betting is a far superior play as the flop is rather scary for mediocre hands such as small pairs. Even against a pair you could have as many as ten outs, which would give you approximately a 40% chance to improve to the winning hand by the river.

Question 4. (a) 10 (b) 2 (c) 0

An incorrigible optimist would see ten outs here, approximately 6-to-1 pot odds, and conclude that it is an easy call. This simplistic assessment is fraught with difficulties. TheRabbit, who we know to be highly timid, has now three-bet out of position, and Madness likes the look of his hand too.

Your only clean out is a jack, and even the J♣ is tainted as it puts a three-flush on board and sets up redraws, even if it doesn't give someone a flush at once. It is time to resign gracefully.

Question 5. (a) 0 (b) 10 (c) 20

You have an easy call as even if you have only seven outs (if TheRabbit has A-Q or K-Q) you are getting pot odds of nearly 10-to-1. However, raising is a far better play. Unless he has an absolute bone-crusher, your three-bet will probably put the frighteners on TheRabbit and get him to shut down. This creates the opportunity to take a free card on the turn or pursue your semi-bluffing strategy. The extra small bet is a cheap price to pay for this.

Question 6. (a) 10 (b) 2 (c) 0

TheRabbit is telling you that he has a very big hand. Please listen. TheRabbit might be a timid player but he is not stupid. He can see that you may easily have a hand as strong as A-Q, but he is telling you that he doesn't care. It is now very likely that your only out is a jack, and the pot odds aren't there to chase it.

Does this mean you made a mistake by three-betting on the flop? No – that is just an illusion. The play cost you an extra $30, but if you had played the hand passively you would still have called the turn with apparently reasonable pot odds, and thus would have spent the $30 there instead.

TheRabbit's response to your three-bet generated the important information that you are way behind in this pot, and enabled you to get away from the hand. Had you played it passively, you may very well have lost even more money if an ace or king came on the river and you called or even raised. When you are facing a player who you are sure will only bet with a very good hand, it is okay to apply pressure and then back off if he plays back at you. This method is more problematic against tough, aggressive opponents as you cannot always be sure where you stand when they give you heat.

Question 7. (a) 7 (b) 10

You have now picked up a flush draw so, unless TheRabbit has a huge hand, you have umpteen outs – possibly as many as 21. The 10 is a great scare card, and it is a good idea to pursue your semi-bluff here, since a bet may even persuade TheRabbit to fold a mediocre queen. Although it is not likely that TheRabbit will muck, it is possible. It is certainly well worth making a bet with a small negative expectation in order to give him the chance to go seriously wrong.

Turn: Q♠-10♣-4♣-8♥. You hold A♠-K♠.

Question 8. (a) 10 (b) 3

The 8♥ may have helped TheRabbit. If he has Q-J or Q-9 he has picked up a gutshot draw (if he holds Q-9 he is not to know that a jack will give you a higher straight) or with Q-8 has made two pair. Even if he hasn't improved, he will have no reason to suspect that the 8♥ has helped you. Thus a bet is unlikely to get him to fold, and he may even raise. Taking a free card is the best option.

River: Q♠-10♣-4♣-8♥-J♣. You hold A♠-K♠.

Question 9. (a) 0 (b) 4 (c) 10

Well, he could have a flush, but it is not that likely on the play. TheRabbit is not the kind of player to check-raise you on the flop with a drawing hand. He sees no reason why you should have a 9 in your hand and is betting his hand for value.

Question 10. (a) 10 (b) 2

The four to a straight is a red herring as it is hard to see why you should have a 9 in your hand. However, your play is consistent with having a flush draw yourself, and this would have come home on the river. TheRabbit's bet is a classic river mistake in that he is making a bet which is unlikely to be called by a losing hand.

♣ – ♥ – ♦ – ♠ – ♣ – ♥ – ♦ – ♠

TIP: One of the most common scenarios in hold'em is that you raise pre-flop with your lovely big cards and then ... miss the flop completely. It is difficult to play accurately with just overcards, as you can rarely be sure where you stand. However, mastering this element of the game is critical to your success.

Hand 3

Rock Crushing

♣ — ♥ — ♦ — ♠ — ♣ — ♥ — ♦ — ♠

INTRODUCTION

This is an eight-player $15-$30 game. You are in the cut-off with A♠-J♥. The button is MrRock, an exceptionally solid, but fortunately also passive, player. MrRock is well known to you. He is a small winner on the site, but this is mainly because other players do not realise how incredibly tight he is and often give him good action on his hands. Even with pretty decent hands he tends to just call. Any time he raises you need something special to compete. However, he does not bluff, so you usually know where you are with him. MrRock has only joined the game in the last few minutes.

The big blind is Volcano. Volcano is a maniac who has been bubbling away for the last hour or so. You have run into Volcano before. He is the archetypal raise or fold player. He hates to call. Any time he is in, he wants to maximise his chances by trying to get everyone else out. Again, this is a strategy that can be successful against players unfamiliar with his style, but you are well used to it.

THE PLAY

Pre-flop

It is passed around to you. There is $25 in the pot and it is $15 to call.

Question 1. Do you: (a) fold (b) call (c) raise?

| (a) ☐ | (b) ☐ | (c) ☐ | Points: .... |

You raise and MrRock now three-bets. This is bad news. MrRock is not one to mess about in such situations. He either has at least a decent pair or a big ace.

The small blind folds and Volcano, true to form, now caps the betting. In principle, the big blind would need a fairly major hand to make such a play, but you are familiar enough with Volcano to know that he does not necessarily have such a holding. All you can be sure of is that he has some sort of hand, which may be big but could equally well be one that does not justify calling two bets cold, let alone raising.

There is now $145 in the pot and it is $30 to you.

Question 2. Do you: (a) fold (b) call?

(a) ☐ (b) ☐	Points: ....

You call as does MrRock. There is $190 in the pot.

Flop

The flop is 2♣-7♠-7♥. You hold A♠-J♥.

This flop certainly hasn't helped you, but it may very well not have helped anyone else either. Unsurprisingly, Volcano now bets out. There is $205 in the pot and it is $15 to you.

Question 3. Do you: (a) fold (b) call (c) raise?

(a) ☐ (b) ☐ (c) ☐	Points: ....

You call.

Hypothetical Play

MrRock now raises and Volcano three-bets. There is $280 in the pot and it is $30 to you.

Question 4. Do you: (a) fold (b) call (c) raise?

(a) ☐ (b) ☐ (c) ☐	Points: ....

Actual Play

MrRock just calls.

Turn

The turn brings 2♣-7♠-7♥-10♦. You hold A♠-J♥.

34

Volcano bets. There is $265 in the pot and it is $30 to you.

Question 5. Do you: (a) fold (b) call (c) raise?

(a) ☐	(b) ☐	(c) ☐	Points: ....

You raise.

MrRock now thinks for a while but, much to your delight, he folds. Volcano doesn't think for very long at all and also folds. You take down a $265 pot with ace-high. Well done!

Hypothetical Play

MrRock folds but Volcano just calls. There is now $355 in the pot. What do you do in the following situations?

Question 6a. The river is 2♣-7♠-7♥-10♦-3♥. You hold A♠-J♥.

Volcano checks. Do you (a) check (b) bet?

(a) ☐	(b) ☐	Points: ....

Question 6b. The river 2♣-7♠-7♥-10♦-10♥. You hold A♠-J♥.

Volcano now bets. Do you (a) fold (b) call (c) raise?

(a) ☐	(b) ☐	(c) ☐	Points: ....

Question 6c. The river is 2♣-7♠-7♥-10♦-J♦. You hold A♠-J♥.

Volcano now bets. Do you (a) fold (b) call (c) raise?

(a) ☐	(b) ☐	(c) ☐	Points: ....
			Total: ....

♣ — ♥ — ♦ — ♠ — ♣ — ♥ — ♦ — ♠

SCORECHART

100   Excellent. You are prepared to take chances, make plays and give opponents heat. You will be a troublesome opponent at the poker table.

90-99   Very good. Please don't sit down in my games.

80-89   Good. A solid performance.

70-79   Average. You need to think more about how your opponents play and how to create problems for them.

60-69   Having a solid player and a maniac in the same hand is never easy to handle.

below 60   Poor.

♣ — ♥ — ♦ — ♠ — ♣ — ♥ — ♦ — ♠

ANSWERS AND ANALYSIS

Holding: A♠-J♥.

Question 1. (a) 0 (b) 1 (c) 5

If you don't raise here you are not going to make any money playing limit hold'em. It is likely you have the best hand, so you must try to take possession of the button and make the blinds pay to play.

Question 2. (a) 3 (b) 10

This has all turned rather ugly. You are not overly concerned about Volcano, but it is very likely that MrRock dominates your hand with a holding such as A-K, A-Q, A-A, K-K or Q-Q. If you are lucky he may have 'only' something like 10-10 or 9-9, when you have two overcards. He also has position on you. Nevertheless, you are getting better than 5-to-1 pot odds to see the flop.

Flop: 2♣-7♠-7♥. You hold A♠-J♥.

Question 3. (a) 7 (b) 20 (c) 12

You are not in great shape in this pot but, nevertheless, folding is rather feeble. The pot has already become large, and you are getting almost 14-to-1 if you just call.

Raising to put pressure on MrRock is a reasonable play. However, if he just calls you will not be any the wiser about his holding, as he is likely to make such a play (and not raise) with anything less than a very big pair. Although he may not realise that Volcano is a maniac, he will still call with A-K or A-Q as he will think that, if nothing else, he has decent pot

36

odds to improve.

These situations are usually raise or fold decisions, but here just calling has a lot to be said for it. You get to stay in the pot cheaply. If MrRock and Volcano now take off, you can resign gracefully. If MrRock just calls, you can be pretty sure that he does not have a bone-crusher and you get to see the turn.

Question 4. (a) 10 (b) 2 (c) 0

You are badly behind here, and will be lucky if you are playing as many as three outs. The normally taciturn MrRock is prepared to raise and Volcano, although a maniac, has now twice re-raised out of position. Your pot odds are about 9-to-1 so you need five good outs for a call. You just don't have them.

Turn: 2♣-7♠-7♥-10♦. You hold A♠-J♥.

Question 5. (a) 20 (b) 6 (c) 30

Calling now is horrible. MrRock will also call with his hand, which is probably beating yours. Folding is not a bad play, but raising is an excellent bluff/semi-bluff. There is a decent chance that your hand is better than Volcano's, and your raise may well get MrRock to fold hands such as A-K, A-Q or even 9-9 and 8-8. If he has an overpair or if he has paired the 10 he will obviously at least call and you will be in trouble. However, he would most likely have raised on the flop with an overpair. You are betting $60 to win $265, so even if your play succeeds just one time in five it will show a profit. An important point here is that MrRock has only recently joined the game and therefore probably does not realise that Volcano is steaming. When you raise he will probably conclude that he needs a seriously big hand to compete, and he may well not have one.

Question 6a. (a) 5 (b) 0

You are most unlikely to get called by a hand you can beat. If he has A-K or A-Q he will be calling. Just check and hope for the best.

Question 6b. (a) 0 (b) 5 (c) 0

This sudden bet from Volcano, after only calling your turn raise, smells very strange. It is possible he has a low pair, such as 5-5, and you have just outdrawn him. In that case he has nothing at all to show down and is launching a desperate bluff. There is no point whatsoever in raising.

Question 6c. (a) 0 (b) 8 (c) 15

You may be splitting the pot here or you will be winning if Volcano has been pumping away with K-J or Q-J. Your turn raise suggested you had made a pair of 10s, so Volcano would have been justified in calling with two overcards, due to the great pot odds he was getting. It is difficult to believe you are now losing unless he has specifically J-10. Even then, he may just call, afraid that you have a 7 in your hand. Raising is the percentage play here – it will win money far more often than it loses.

Many players may well be highly sceptical of your play in this hand. Your turn raise is certainly a considerable gamble, as you almost certainly do not have the best hand at that point and you don't really have many outs against a better one. However, in a sense your cards are actually somewhat irrelevant. You are making a play based on your knowledge of the state of mind and styles of the players at the table, and your actual holding is almost a secondary consideration. Anyway, what would be the point of playing poker if you never tried to win a pot with the worse hand?

However, please be aware that conditions have to be absolutely right for a play like this to be worthwhile. This is not a play you make three or four times a session; it is more like a play you might try once every thousand or so hands.

♣ – ♥ – ♦ – ♠ – ♣ – ♥ – ♦ – ♠

TIP: Sometimes you need to focus on playing the players rather than the cards.

Hand 4

Danger Ahead

♣ — ♥ — ♦ — ♠ — ♣ — ♥ — ♦ — ♠

INTRODUCTION

This is a nine-player $20-$40 game. You are in the big blind with A♠-6♠. Charlie, a fairly soft, loose player, is in middle position. He doesn't show much aggression, gets involved too often without sufficient values and often sticks around longer than is justified. The cut-off is Dangerous. Dangerous is a tight/aggressive player, but not a very sophisticated one. He is the complete opposite of Charlie: he doesn't get involved often, but if he does, he is usually betting and raising. If the game were full of players like Dangerous, you wouldn't bother with it.

THE PLAY

Pre-flop

Hypothetical Play

Let's switch the players round: Dangerous is now in middle position and opens with a raise. Charlie is in the cut-off and calls two bets cold. The button and small blind fold. There is $110 in the pot and it is $20 to you.

Question 1. Do you: (a) fold (b) call (c) raise?

| (a) ☐ | (b) ☐ | (c) ☐ | Points: .... |

Hypothetical Play

The situation is as above, but now you hold A♠-6♥.

Question 2. Do you: (a) fold (b) call (c) raise?

> (a) ☐   (b) ☐   (c) ☐   Points: ....

Actual Play

Charlie limps in. It is passed around to Dangerous, who raises. The button and small blind muck. There is $90 in the pot and it is $20 to you.

Question 3. Do you: (a) fold (b) call (c) raise?

> (a) ☐   (b) ☐   (c) ☐   Points: ....

You call. Charlie also calls.

Question 4. Regardless of your actual answers, are you more inclined to get involved in the pot with the scenario outlined in (a) Question 1 (b) Question 3?

> (a) ☐   (b) ☐   Points: ....

Flop

The flop is 8♣-6♦-3♠. You hold A♠-6♠.

Hypothetical Play

Let us assume that the play is as for Question 1 with Dangerous in middle position and Charlie in the cut-off. There is $130 in the pot and it is $20 to you.

Question 5. Do you: (a) check, planning a check-raise (b) check, planning to call (c) bet?

> (a) ☐   (b) ☐   (c) ☐   Points: ....

Actual Play

As you were now, with Charlie limping pre-flop from middle position and Dangerous raising from the cut-off. There is $130 in the pot and it is $20 to you.

Question 6. Do you: (a) check, planning a check-raise (b) check, awaiting developments (c) bet?

> (a) ☐   (b) ☐   (c) ☐   Points: ....

You check. Charlie also checks and Dangerous bets. There is $150 in the pot and it is $20 to you.

Question 7. Do you: (a) fold (b) call (c) raise?

(a) ☐   (b) ☐   (c) ☐   Points: ....

You raise. Charlie now folds and Dangerous just calls.

Turn

The turn is . You hold A♠-6♠.

There is $210 in the pot and it is $40 to bet.

Question 8. Do you: (a) check, planning a check-raise (b) check, planning to call (c) bet?

(a) ☐   (b) ☐   (c) ☐   Points: ....

You bet. Dangerous now raises. There is $330 in the pot and it is $40 to you.

Question 9. Do you: (a) fold (b) call (c) raise?

(a) ☐   (b) ☐   (c) ☐   Points: ....

You raise and Dangerous calls.

River

The river is 8♣-6♦-3♠-A♥-8♥. You hold A♠-6♠.

There is $450 in the pot and it is $40 to bet.

Question 10. Do you (a) check (b) bet?

(a) ☐   (b) ☐   Points: ....

You check and Dangerous now bets. There is $490 in the pot and it is $40 to you.

Question 11. Do you: (a) fold (b) call (c) raise?

(a) ☐   (b) ☐   (c) ☐   Points: ....

                                   Total: ....

You call. Dangerous now shows you A♣-Q♠ and takes the pot thanks to the queen kicker.

♣ — ♥ — ♦ — ♠ — ♣ — ♥ — ♦ — ♠

SCORECHART

100   Excellent. Skilful play in uncertain conditions with a mediocre holding.

90-99   Very good. You squeezed very nearly the maximum from your holding.

80-89   Good.

70-79   Average. You need to focus more on how to achieve your aims and how likely your hand is to be good.

60-69   You may have been too passive in questions 8 and 9. With big hands you need to extract the most you possibly can from your opponents.

below 60   Poor.

♣ — ♥ — ♦ — ♠ — ♣ — ♥ — ♦ — ♠

ANSWERS AND ANALYSIS

Holding: A♠-6♠.

Question 1. (a) 10 (b) 7 (c) 0

You don't have a great hand, but it is only $20 to see the flop with reasonable pot odds. You will have to be very careful if an ace flops and somebody else gets excited, as you have no kicker. It is probably best to fold, but seeing the flop is not terrible.

Question 2. (a) 10 (b) 3 (c) 0

Making the hand offsuit makes a big difference here. You are now quite likely to be dominated, and your only really decent flop is two pair or a miracle such as 6-6. If an ace flops it may very well just cost you money. It is best to dump the hand.

Question 3. (a) 2 (b) 5 (c) 0

This is now an easy call. Charlie only limped originally, so he could have any old rubbish. Dangerous – who knows Charlie plays some garbage hands – would likely raise with more or less any hand he wanted to play, so your ace may even be best.

Question 4. (a) 1 (b) 5

The betting to date suggests that both of your opponents have stronger hands in the Question 1 scenario than Question 3. Dangerous is open-raising from a worse position, and Charlie is calling two bets cold rather than limping.

Flop: 8♣-6♦-3♠. You hold A♠-6♠.

Question 5. (a) 7 (b) 2 (c) 10

There is a good chance that you are winning here and the priority is to find the best way to protect your hand. If you check, Dangerous will probably bet, and then Charlie will have a fairly easy call even with just random overcards. You could then raise, which would announce a strong hand and get more money into the pot, but it wouldn't get anyone out.

Betting is a superior play. Since Dangerous is so aggressive, it is quite likely that he will raise, making it difficult for Charlie to compete if he has not connected with the flop. You can then (at least) call, secure in the knowledge that by elbowing Charlie out, your chances of winning the pot have increased.

Question 6. (a) 20 (b) 5 (c) 12

Planning a check-raise is now the best way to put pressure on Charlie. Charlie will probably check, Dangerous will bet and then you can check-raise.

Question 7. (a) 0 (b) 1 (c) 5

As planned.

Turn: 8♣-6♦-3♠-A♥. You hold A♠-6♠.

Question 8. (a) 8 (b) 4 (c) 20

You have a hit a major hand, and it is now time to decide how to extract the most bets from your opponent. Since we know that Dangerous is aggressive, the best plan is to bet out in the hope that he has connected with the ace. He will then likely raise, and we can three-bet him. This strategy has a good chance of success and scores an extra bet over the simple check-raise.

Checking also runs the risk that Dangerous may simply check it back and take a free card. If he is playing a big pair, you have given him a free chance to make a hand.

Question 9. (a) 0 (b) 2 (c) 5

It is very likely you are winning here, but you can easily be outdrawn. You must make Dangerous pay the maximum for the privilege.

River: 8♣-6♦-3♠-A♥-8♥. You hold A♠-6♠.

Question 10. (a) 5 (b) 0

Yuk! The 8♥ has destroyed your holding as it has wiped out your second pair. It is now highly likely that you are losing. Betting here is ridiculous.

Question 11. (a) 3 (b) 5 (c) 0

It is hard to justify not making a crying call, as the pot odds are enormous. Perhaps Dangerous has been trying it on, although this doesn't seem very likely.

♣ — ♥ — ♦ — ♠ — ♣ — ♥ — ♦ — ♠

TIP: When you hit a big hand against a soft weak player it is sometimes best to check in the hope of check-raising. However, when facing a good aggressive player you need to think differently. These tough players are more likely to play back at you, so betting out and hoping for a raise can often be a superior strategy.

Hand 5

Sharp Teeth

INTRODUCTION

This is a six-player $15-$30 game. You are on the button with A♣-8♥. Tiger is in the big blind. Tiger is a decent player who is very aggressive without being a maniac. He plays fairly loosely and is a big bluffer and semi-bluffer. You can get the better of Tiger, because he is too loose, but he is very tricky and is much easier to play in a full ring game than short-handed, as here.

THE PLAY

Pre-flop

It is passed around to you. There is $25 in the pot and it is $15 to you.

Question 1. Do you: (a) fold (b) call (c) raise?

(a) ☐   (b) ☐   (c) ☐   Points: ....

You raise.

Hypothetical Pre-flop

Let us assume that you are a good, aggressive player and would have open-raised on the button with any of the following holdings: A♣-8♥ (as you actually hold), Q♦-J♠ and 2♣-2♠.

Question 2. Which of these hands would you actually prefer to hold in this position: (a) your actual holding, A♣-8♥ (b) Q♦-J♠ (c) 2♣-2♠?

(a) ☐   (b) ☐   (c) ☐   Points: ....

Actual Play

As we know, your real holding is A♣-8♥ and you have open-raised.

Hypothetical Play

The small blind folds and Tiger now three-bets. There is $85 in the pot and it is $15 to you.

Question 3. Do you: (a) fold (b) call (c) raise?

(a) ☐   (b) ☐   (c) ☐   Points: ....

Actual Play

The small blinds folds and Tiger calls.

Flop

The flop is an agreeable one for you, A♦-9♣-2♣. You hold A♣-8♥.

Tiger checks. There is $70 in the pot and it is $15 to bet.

Question 4. Do you: (a) bet (b) check?

(a) ☐   (b) ☐   Points: ....

You bet and Tiger raises. There is $115 in the pot and it is $15 to you.

Hypothetical Play

Let us assume that play in the hand to date has been exactly the same, but that your opponent in the big blind is not Tiger but the softer player Charlie who we met in Hand 4. There is $115 in the pot and it is $15 to you. How do you respond to Charlie's raise?

Question 5. Do you: (a) fold (b) call (c) raise?

(a) ☐   (b) ☐   (c) ☐   Points: ....

Actual Play

We have now removed the phantom Charlie from the big blind seat, and replaced him with his more aggressive counterpart, Tiger. There is $115 in the pot and it is $15 to you. How do you respond to Tiger's raise?

Question 6. Do you: (a) fold (b) call (c) raise?

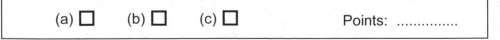

(a) ☐   (b) ☐   (c) ☐   Points: ....

You call.

Turn

Hypothetical Turn

The turn is A♦-9♣-2♣-A♥. You hold A♣-8♥.

Tiger now bets. There is $160 in the pot and it is $30 to you.

Question 7. Do you: (a) fold (b) call (c) raise?

(a) ☐ (b) ☐ (c) ☐	Points: ....

Actual Turn

The turn is A♦-9♣-2♣-3♣. You hold A♣-8♥. Tiger now bets. There is $160 in the pot and it is $30 to you.

Question 8. Do you: (a) fold (b) call (c) raise?

(a) ☐ (b) ☐ (c) ☐	Points: ....

You raise.

Hypothetical Play

Tiger now three-bets. There is $280 in the pot and it is $30 to you.

Question 9. Do you: (a) fold (b) call (c) raise?

(a) ☐ (b) ☐ (c) ☐	Points: ....

Actual Play

Tiger just calls.

River

The river is A♦-9♣-2♣-3♣-K♥. You hold A♣-8♥.

Tiger checks. There is $250 in the pot and it is $30 to bet.

Question 10. Do you: (a) bet (b) check

(a) ☐ (b) ☐	Points: ....
	Total: ....

You check and Tiger shows you A♠-2♠, taking the pot with two pair.

♣ — ♥ — ♦ — ♠ — ♣ — ♥ — ♦ — ♠

SCORECHART

100   Excellent. Heads-up pots require good reading of the opponent and you showed that here.

90-99   Very good.

80-89   Good. You may need to focus more on what you know about your opponent.

70-79   Average.

60-69   Short-handed play is difficult. You may be better off in full ring games.

below 60 Poor.

♣ — ♥ — ♦ — ♠ — ♣ — ♥ — ♦ — ♠

ANSWERS AND ANALYSIS

Holding: A♣-8♥.

Question 1. (a) 0 (b) 2 (c) 10

Your holding is not magnificent, but it is quite sufficient to open-raise from the button against two random hands. Someone will need a pretty decent holding to dominate you.

Question 2. (a) 12 (b) 20 (c) 4

Strangely, it is the weakest actual hand that offers the best playing chances. Let us see why this is so. First, if both blinds fold, it obviously does not matter what you hold, or even if you look at your cards for that matter. So let us assume that you get called (or even raised) in at least one spot.

The following scenario is the most likely. You are called by just one player, the flop comes, they check and you bet, whether the flop hit you or not. If they now fold, again it makes no difference what cards you have, so we will have to assume that they at least call. The hardest hand to play properly now is the pair of twos. It is unlikely that you would have flopped a set, so you have to decide if your opponent has called (or raised) with a pair, a draw or maybe just overcards. You may well feel obliged to keep firing at the pot when you are losing and playing just two outs. Limit hold'em is all about avoiding mistakes, and in situations like these, that becomes very difficult.

If you have A♣-8♥, the hand is easier to play. If you have made a pair you will very likely at least call to the river and may well decide to take more aggressive action. If you have no pair and the board features high cards, you will probably decide you are playing just three outs and might well just give it up.

However, the best hand is Q♦-J♠. If you have made a pair you are in great shape. If you have no pair and there is an overcard, you will probably give up, and this will be a relatively easy decision. If you have two overcards you probably have six outs (and maybe even ten if you have picked up a gutshot as well). You may then even take an aggressive posture in the hand.

Furthermore, Q♦-J♠ is a hand that is more likely to get paid off. For example, if the big blind calls with 6♣-7♣ and the flop is Q♥-7♥-2♦ you could get good action and win a decent pot. However, if you hold A♣-8♥ and the flop is A♥-7♥-2♦, your opponent will probably be more circumspect as he will 'expect' you to have an ace in your hand.

Although Q♦-J♠ is the weakest of the three hands it is the best *playing* hand. In short-handed pots it has more energy than the other holdings, is more likely to get paid off, and less likely to cause you to make mistakes.

Question 3. (a) 0 (b) 5 (c) 1

Tiger's three-bet is not great news, but there is no reason not to see the flop. Escalating the pot with such a mediocre holding also would be silly.

Flop: A♦-9♣-2♣. You hold A♣-8♥.

Question 4. (a) 5 (b) 0

You are very likely winning and there is no excuse for not betting. Heads-up, some players might like to 'slowplay' such a hand and just check, hoping to elicit a bet on the turn from a weak hand. If you are playing a heads-up match this would have some merit, as it would be vital to vary your play. However, in a ring game this is poor play.

Question 5. (a) 2 (b) 7 (c) 10

Against Charlie it is probably best to re-raise. This raise is likely to make Charlie back down, and it may well enable you to take a free card on the turn if you wish. It is not certain that Charlie is beating you, and it is important to keep the initiative.

Question 6. (a) 0 (b) 10 (c) 7

You are heads-up and have top pair, so you are not going to muck – at least I hope not. Tiger's raise could be made with a wide range of hands. Against such an aggressive opponent I prefer to just call and see the turn. If you re-raise, he may well cap the betting and then lead out on the turn.

Assuming the turn is a blank, you would then have to muck, but he may have pushed you off the winning hand.

Question 7. (a) 0 (b) 4 (c) 10

You might be losing, but now that another ace has appeared, it doesn't seem very likely. If Tiger has a better ace then he is playing at least A-T, and with such a hand he would probably have three-bet pre-flop. Of course there are other hands he could hold which might be winning, e.g. A-9, A-2, 9-9 and 2-2, but these are not all that likely. Tiger would probably wait for the turn to check-raise with such big hands. It is much more probable that he has two clubs or possibly a weaker ace.

Turn: A♦-9♣-2♣-3♣. You hold A♣-8♥.

Question 8. (a) 0 (b) 10 (c) 15

It is a close decision, but raising looks like the better play. There is a fair chance you are winning the hand, and you still have a decent number of outs even if Tiger does have a flush or a better made hand, such as two pair.

Question 9. (a) 0 (b) 5 (c) 0

Okay, you need to improve, but even if you are up against a made flush you have seven outs (barring an unlikely straight flush) and easily have pot odds to call.

River: A♦-9♣-2♣-3♣-K♥. You hold A♣-8♥.

Question 10. (a) 3 (b) 10

You have a classic free showdown – it is best to take it. Note that your turn raise did not cost anything, as you would have paid two big bets to call Tiger down in any case. Playing aggressively on the turn gave you extra opportunities to win the hand (Tiger may have folded a less impressive holding) and also created the chance to win a further big bet if you improved on the river.

If you have scored highly on Hands 4 and 5 then you have played very well and have absolutely nothing to show for it. When this happens in your real games do *not* let it affect your play. It is perfectly possible to play seemingly endless amounts of excellent poker and end up with a big deficit in your bankroll.

It may sound rather strange, but the most important thing to achieve when playing poker is *not* to win money. It is to constantly make the correct decisions. Winning money is actually secondary. If you can consistently play good poker – whether the cards are running for you or not – then the money will take care of itself. This may take a while. It is possible to run badly not just for two hands, but for many thousands. You have to be patient.

This is one of the hardest poker lessons to learn. You can find good tables with weak opponents, play your 'A' game and yet lose money for many weeks. However, if you really are better than your opponents, and you have the self-discipline to see out these long barren periods, then things will eventually go your way. The Gods of Mathematics have decreed it. So heed them ... and don't go on tilt.

♣ — ♥ — ♦ — ♠ — ♣ — ♥ — ♦ — ♠

 TIP: Short-handed and heads-up play is very different from full ring game play, especially when, as here, the players have entered the pot from late positions. Hand values change enormously and concentrating upon the style of your opponent becomes crucial.

Hand 6

Trash

♣ — ♥ — ♦ — ♠ — ♣ — ♥ — ♦ — ♠

INTRODUCTION

This is a nine-player $15-$30 game. You are in the big blind with the exciting 7♥-4♣. This is a good game to be in. The players are all rather loose and passive, and there is hardly any pre-flop raising. Most pots are contested with four or five players seeing the flop for a single bet. You have had no cards at all in the game, and your current holding is fairly typical of what has come your way.

THE PLAY

Pre-flop

Hypothetical Play 1

You are in the small blind rather than the big blind. An early player limps and a middle player calls. There is $55 in the pot and it is $5 to you to call, or $20 if you fancy a raise.

Question 1. Do you (a) fold (b) call (c) raise?

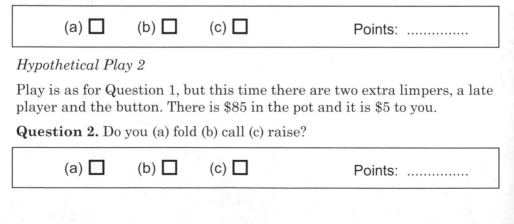

(a) ☐   (b) ☐   (c) ☐   Points: ....

Hypothetical Play 2

Play is as for Question 1, but this time there are two extra limpers, a late player and the button. There is $85 in the pot and it is $5 to you.

Question 2. Do you (a) fold (b) call (c) raise?

(a) ☐   (b) ☐   (c) ☐   Points: ....

Actual Play

After this small game of musical chairs you now relocate yourself into the correct seat – the big blind. An early player limps, a middle player calls, as does the small blind. There is $60 in the pot. You can check or it is $15 to raise.

Question 3. Do you (a) check (b) raise?

(a) ☐   (b) ☐   Points: ....

Flop

Hypothetical Flop 1

The flop is K♠-10♥-4♠. You hold 7♥-4♣.

The small blind checks. There is $60 in the pot and it is $15 to bet.

Question 4. Do you (a) check (b) bet?

(a) ☐   (b) ☐   Points: ....

Hypothetical Flop 2

The flop is K♣-7♥-2♠. You hold 7♥-4♣.

The small blind checks. There is $60 in the pot and it is $15 to bet.

Question 5. Do you (a) check (b) bet?

(a) ☐   (b) ☐   Points: ....

Hypothetical Flop 3

The flop is 5♠-6♥-K♣. You hold 7♥-4♣.

The small blind checks. Betting your open draw here is fine, but you decide to check. The early player checks and the middle player bets. The small blind folds. There is $75 in the pot and it is $15 to you.

Question 6. Do you (a) fold (b) call (c) raise?

(a) ☐   (b) ☐   (c) ☐   Points: ....

Actual Flop

The flop is Q♥-8♣-2♠. You hold 7♥-4♣.

The small blind checks. There is $60 in the pot and it is $15 to bet.

Question 7. Do you (a) check (b) bet?

(a) ☐   (b) ☐   Points: ....

You check, as do both other players.

Turn

The turn is Q♥-8♣-2♠-2♦. You hold 7♥-4♣.

The small blind checks. There is $60 in the pot and it is $30 to bet.

Question 8. Do you (a) check (b) bet?

(a) ☐   (b) ☐   Points: ....

You bet.

Hypothetical Play

The early player calls and both others fold. The river is Q♥-8♣-2♠-2♦-J♣. You hold 7♥-4♣.

There is $120 in the pot and it is $30 to bet.

Question 9. Do you (a) check (b) bet?

(a) ☐   (b) ☐   Points: ....

                                          Total: ....

Actual Play

Everyone folds on the turn and you take down a $60 pot. Well done! If you are a good player, expecting to make one big bet per hour, then you have just earned two hours' pay.

♣ — ♥ — ♦ — ♠ — ♣ — ♥ — ♦ — ♠

SCORECHART

100   Excellent. You are an accomplished thief.

90-99   Very good. Please keep your kleptomaniac tendencies away from my games.

80-89   Good. It is important to spot these stealing opportunities.

70-79   Average. Quite often no-one has anything, but someone still has to get the money. Make sure that you get at least a fair share of these pots.

60-69   You are far too honest for your own good. An admirable quality, but not terribly helpful for your poker career.

below 60   Poor.

♣ – ♥ – ♦ – ♠ – ♣ – ♥ – ♦ – ♠

ANSWERS AND ANALYSIS

Holding: 7♥-4♣.

Question 1. (a) 7 (b) 10 (c) 0

Assuming that the big blind does not raise – and the character of the game makes this likely – you are getting 11-to-1 for your $5. However, your hand is so awful that this only just represents good value. Change it to 7♥-6♣ and you can call with enthusiasm. However, you have to play the hand well – which means mucking it and not paying off if you make a mediocre hand, which is very likely going to be second best.

The main reason to call here is not that you are particularly fond of your cards or even that they are likely to generate a natural winning hand. The point is that you actually get to stay in the pot. This, in itself, has some value. Even if the game permitted you to be dealt two blank cards – so that you could never make any hand at all – it would still be worth calling for this reason. There are a number of flops that can allow you a decent stab at an immediate steal by simply betting out. For example K-6-2 rainbow is unlikely to have connected with anyone. A bet now – even with the hypothetical blank cards – is likely to have a positive expectation.

Question 2. (a) 5 (b) 10 (c) 0

Now you are getting 17-to-1, which is quite different from 11-to-1. You are 3.5% to make two pair, trips or something even better and this, combined with the chance of flopping an open-ended straight draw, makes a call justified. However, mucking is still not bad as even if you hit a miracle two pair, they will be so feeble that they may well struggle to stand up in a multi-way pot.

Question 3. (a) 5 (b) 0

This is about as close to a no-brainer as it gets.

Question 4. (a) 10 (b) 3

Your hand is too feeble to justify a bet. Anyone with a king or a 10 is certain to, at the very least, call. There are also various straight draw and gutshot possibilities. Furthermore, the two-flush slightly harms your chances, as anyone with a flush draw will probably raise, and your hand cannot take any heat at all. If the flop has completely missed everyone you might take it, but given its texture, this is not very likely.

Question 5. (a) 5 (b) 10

This is more like it, and now a bet is justified. There is only one overcard and there is no hint of a draw anywhere. If you get heat you can fold safely, and if no-one has a king – and there is a fair chance of this – you may take the pot at once.

Question 6. (a) 0 (b) 3 (c) 15

You have hit a very decent hand here and it is time to apply some pressure. The bettor may taking a stab at the pot without so much as a pair, and even if he has one, you have a 32% chance to make a straight by the river. This is an excellent semi-bluff check-raise. You will, of course, keep firing no matter what comes on the turn. One small point here is that he might have paired the 5 or 6 and get obstinate, in which case you have an extra three outs with a 7.

Flop: Q♥-8♣-2♠. You hold 7♥-4♣.

Question 7. (a) 5 (b) 2

You could have a go at it, but the two high cards are just slightly too close together to justify it. Change the Q-8 combination to Q-6 and a bet becomes more justifiable.

Turn: Q♥-8♣-2♠-2♦. You hold 7♥-4♣.

Question 8. (a) 5 (b) 25

There is $60 sitting in the pot rotting away and someone has to take it. If the players here were more aggressive it would be prudent to be circumspect. However, they are all passive players and nobody was interested on the flop – it is very unlikely that pairing the 2 will have excited anyone. Note that it has not even created a two-flush, so you won't get a call from a flush draw. It is a bad error to check here in this type of game –

you are getting 2-to-1 for a bet and you will probably take the money at least 50% of the time.

Question 9. (a) 10 (b) 2

Let it go. I know it is a bit feeble, but firing another $30 here cannot really be justified. It is almost impossible to construct a hand that your opponent could have where they will not call. If they were calling because they thought they might have the best made hand (even if it is only, say A-10 or 3-3), they will certainly call on the river. The only possible draw was a gutshot with two cards between the queen and the 8. If this is the case, then their hand has improved to, at the very least, a pair of jacks, and there is no way they are going to muck that.

♣ — ♥ — ♦ — ♠ — ♣ — ♥ — ♦ — ♠

TIP: When you receive yet another in an apparently end-less stream of trash hands, there is a great temptation to activate the 'auto-fold' button, get up and put the kettle on. Resist it. If the conditions are right, you can take down a hold'em pot with any hand. However, if your mind is elsewhere you will miss these opportunities and your bankroll will suffer.

Hand 7

Dennis the Menace

♣ — ♥ — ♦ — ♠ — ♣ — ♥ — ♦ — ♠

INTRODUCTION

This is a ten-player $15-$30 game. You are in middle position with A♣-K♥. The cut-off is Tortoise, who is a completely awful player. Tortoise often gets busy with bets and raises with woefully inadequate values. At the same time, when he hits a big hand, he often crawls into his shell, and is inclined to slowplay his hand to such an extent that you can barely see him move. Occasionally he gets an adrenalin rush and launches a huge bluff – usually when there are about nine other players in the pot. Heads-up he is easy to play against, but because of his unpredictability he causes trouble in multi-way pots – not, however, by actually having a decent hand and winning them. The small blind is Dennis, who is a good player. The big blind is Athens – of whom you know nothing.

THE PLAY

Pre-flop

It is folded round to you. There is $25 in the pot and it is $15 to you.

Question 1. Do you (a) fold (b) call (c) raise?

(a) ☐   (b) ☐   (c) ☐   Points: ....

You raise.

Hypothetical Play

Tortoise calls as does Dennis. Athens now pops up with a re-raise. There is $135 in the pot and it is $15 to you.

Question 2. Do you (a) fold (b) call (c) raise?

(a) ☐   (b) ☐   (c) ☐   Points: ....

Actual Play

Tortoise, Dennis and Athens all call.

Flop

The flop is A♦-5♥-J♦. You hold A♣-K♥.

Dennis and Athens check. There is $120 in the pot and it is $15 to bet.

Question 3. Do you (a) check (b) bet?

(a) ☐   (b) ☐   Points: ....

You bet.

Tortoise leaps in with a raise, and Dennis thinks for a while and finally calls. Athens gives up. There is $195 in the pot and it is $15 to you.

Question 4. Do you (a) fold (b) call (c) raise?

(a) ☐   (b) ☐   (c) ☐   Points: ....

You raise and both players call.

Turn

The turn is A♦-5♥-J♦-10♣. You hold A♣-K♥.

Dennis checks. There is $255 in the pot and it is $30 to bet.

Question 5. Do you (a) check (b) bet?

(a) ☐   (b) ☐   Points: ....

You bet. Tortoise now raises. Dennis again thinks for a while and calls. There is $405 in the pot and it is $30 to you.

Question 6. Do you (a) fold (b) call (c) raise?

(a) ☐   (b) ☐   (c) ☐   Points: ....

You call.

River

The river is A♦-5♥-J♦-10♣-2♣. You hold A♣-K♥.

Dennis checks. There is $435 in the pot and it is $30 to bet.

Question 7. Do you (a) check (b) bet?

(a) ☐   (b) ☐   Points: ....

You check and Tortoise bets.

Hypothetical Play

Dennis calls. There is $495 in the pot and it is $30 to you.

Question 8. Do you (a) fold (b) call (c) raise?

(a) ☐   (b) ☐   (c) ☐   Points: ....

Actual Play

Dennis now raises. There is $525 in the pot and it is $60 to you.

Question 9. Do you (a) fold (b) call (c) raise?

(a) ☐   (b) ☐   (c) ☐   Points: ....

You fold. Tortoise calls. Dennis shows K♣-Q♣ for a made straight on the turn. The hand history shows that Tortoise had A♥-10♠.

Dennis made three decisions worthy of note in this hand:

1) He called on the flop.

2) He only called the turn with the nuts.

3) He played for a check-raise on the river with the nuts.

Question 10. How would you rate Dennis's play in this hand (a) poor (b) reasonable (c) good (d) very good?

(a) ☐   (b) ☐   (c) ☐   (d) ☐   Points: ....

                                                       Total: ....

♣ — ♥ — ♦ — ♠ — ♣ — ♥ — ♦ — ♠

SCORECHART

100	Excellent. The hand was not a happy one for you, but you played it well.
90-99	Very good.
80-89	Good. You got the main points of the deal.
70-79	Average. Maybe you gave in too easily or pushed too hard.
60-69	Never mind. Always keep an eye on the pot size and bear in mind the tendencies of your opponents.
below 60	Poor.

♣ — ♥ — ♦ — ♠ — ♣ — ♥ — ♦ — ♠

ANSWERS AND ANALYSIS

Holding: A♣-K♥.

Question 1. (a) 0 (b) 1 (c) 5

There is nothing to think about here. A-K is a big hand and there is no excuse for limping.

Question 2. (a) 0 (b) 10 (c) 6

Obviously you have an easy call, but raising is not recommended. If Athens is a reasonable player then he should have a pretty decent hand for his three-bet out of position. You could argue that a raise might force out either or both of Tortoise and Dennis, but this is not very likely. Also, note that your position on this hand is uncomfortable. On the flop you will more than likely have to respond to a bet from Athens before either Tortoise or Dennis have spoken.

Flop: A♦-5♥-J♦. You hold A♣-K♥.

Question 3. (a) 0 (b) 5

You have top pair, top kicker. Not a lot to think about here. You are probably winning, but there are two high cards on the flop, two diamonds and four players in the pot. Checking with the idea if check-raising is horrible. For a start it might get checked around and secondly, although good, your hand is not really strong enough to check-raise.

Question 4. (a) 0 (b) 7 (c) 10

You should not be overly worried about Tortoise's holding here. You are probably beating him. Dennis called two bets cold and is more of a worry. However, if he were beating you he would probably have three-bet. Simply calling and seeing the turn is not bad, but there is no strong reason to think you are not winning, and therefore a raise is in order.

Turn: A♦-5♥-J♦-10♣. You hold A♣-K♥.

Question 5. (a) 2 (b) 10

The 10 is not a pleasant card, but you must bet now to find out where you stand. If you check here and someone else bets, you still won't know where you are. It is better to keep the initiative with a bet.

Question 6. (a) 8 (b) 20 (c) 0

At first sight it would seem obvious that your position is hopeless and that a fold is in order. You three-bet the flop and led out on the turn, but Tortoise was unimpressed and fired back a raise. We know that Tortoise is a wildly unpredictable player, but even so he must surely be beating us here. Furthermore Dennis, a sensible player, has called two bets cold. It does not look good.

Nevertheless, this pot has got huge and you have enough of a hand to call. You have pot odds of 13½-to-1, and have value even to try for the miracle queen on the river, although there is obviously a danger that this will result in a split pot. On a good day Tortoise 'only' has a two-pair hand, and Dennis is on a flush draw. In that case you have even more outs and an easy call. The problem is that if Tortoise has a made straight with K-Q, then you are playing three outs (at best) to tie. However, the pot is substantial, Tortoise is known to be erratic and Dennis could easily be on a draw. Furthermore, your call closes the betting, so there is no danger of an uncomfortable raise. This is not the time for a tough fold.

River: A♦-5♥-J♦-10♣-2♣. You hold A♣-K♥.

Question 7. (a) 5 (b) 0

If you bet here I advise you to play only for play money.

Question 8. (a) 10 (b) 2 (c) 0

Dennis is a good player and he has called. There is no chance that his hand is weaker than yours. Although you have umpteen-to-1 pot odds, it doesn't matter. You are not getting anything out of this pot and $30 is $30 – throw the hand away.

Question 9. (a) 5 (b) 0 (c) 1

This raise from Dennis is slightly suspicious, but it is still a clear fold for you here. Even if he is trying an outrageous bluff, you still have to beat Tortoise. It is vaguely possible that a raise might work, but it feels like an extreme long shot.

Question 10. (a) 20 (b) 12 (c) 5 (d) 0

Dennis is a good player but, although he scored a good win here, his play of this hand was poor at almost all stages.

1) The initial flop call was very poor. There was $165 in the pot and he paid $30 to call. His only out is a 10 – the pot odds are just not there. There is also a danger that you might re-raise (as indeed you did) forcing him to pay even more for his draw. The two-flush weakens his holding, tainting the 10♦ and creating redraws.

2) Slowplaying the turn by just calling was also very poor. It is obvious what he is trying to do – he is hoping to lure you in for an extra bet, and then is hoping that Tortoise will lead out on the river when a blank comes. This worked out okay in this instance, but it could easily have gone horribly wrong. By just calling, he is giving you pot odds to call with two pair or a flush draw, and is losing extra bets when you have a big hand such as a set. He is also losing sight of a basic principle: when the pot gets big your aim is to win it at all costs and not to mess around trying to finagle an extra bet here or there.

3) Even this play is doubtful and he is lucky that Tortoise fell for his trap.

♣ — ♥ — ♦ — ♠ — ♣ — ♥ — ♦ — ♠

TIP: Always bear in mind the playing style of the opposition. When a 'normal' player raises you on the turn in the above hand, you can be fairly sure you are badly beaten and playing very few outs. However, when the raise comes from a player with a track record of unpredictability, you have to be more circumspect. Furthermore, do not make tough folds when the pot is very large. When you are right, it saves very little; when you are wrong, it is a huge mistake.

Hand 8

Small Blind, Small Hand

♣ — ♥ — ♦ — ♠ — ♣ — ♥ — ♦ — ♠

INTRODUCTION

This is a ten-player $15-$30 game. You are in the small blind with 10♣-9♣. David is sitting in middle position, and George is in the big blind. They are both normal players. John is on the button, and he is a very good player. His pre-flop play is slightly loose and occasionally unconventional. However, his post-flop play is generally excellent.

THE PLAY

Pre-flop

David limps, as does John. There is $55 in the pot and it is $5 to call or $20 to raise.

Hypothetical Play

Your holding of 10♣-9♣ has miraculously transformed into K♣-Q♥.

Question 1. Do you (a) fold (b) call (c) raise?

(a) ☐	(b) ☐	(c) ☐	Points: ....

Actual Play

As you were with 10♣-9♣.

Question 2. Do you (a) fold (b) call (c) raise?

(a) ☐	(b) ☐	(c) ☐	Points: ....

You call. George declines to raise and four of you see the flop.

Flop

The flop is 9♠-6♥-5♠. You hold 10♣-9♣.

There is $60 in the pot and it is $15 to bet.

Hypothetical Play

Let's change the pre-flop play. Assume that David limped and John then raised. Noting the prospect of a decent-sized pot, you decided to call from the small blind and George and David also called. The flop is the same. There is $120 in the pot and it is $15 to you.

Question 3. Do you (a) check, planning to call (b) check, hoping to check-raise (c) bet?

(a) ☐   (b) ☐   (c) ☐   Points: ....

Actual Play

Now we are back with everybody being in for a single bet and a smaller pot size. There is $60 in the pot and it is $15 to bet.

Question 4. Do you (a) check, planning to call (b) check, hoping to check-raise (c) bet?

(a) ☐   (b) ☐   (c) ☐   Points: ....

You bet.

David and George fold and John now raises. There is $105 in the pot and it is $15 to you.

Question 5. Do you (a) fold (b) call (c) raise?

(a) ☐   (b) ☐   (c) ☐   Points: ....

You call.

Turn

The turn is 9♠-6♥-5♠-3♥. You hold 10♣-9♣.

There is $120 in the pot and it is $30 to bet.

65

Question 6. Do you (a) check (b) bet?

(a) ☐   (b) ☐   Points: ....

You bet.

Hypothetical Play

Let us now assume that your opponent here is not the strong player John, but Ben, who is a weak, passive player. Ben now raises. There is $210 in the pot and it is $30 to you.

Question 7. Do you (a) fold (b) call (c) raise?

(a) ☐   (b) ☐   (c) ☐   Points: ....

Actual Play

We are now back with the strong player John. John now thinks for a few moments and then raises. There is $210 in the pot and it is $30 to you.

Question 8. Do you (a) fold (b) call (c) raise?

(a) ☐   (b) ☐   (c) ☐   Points: ....

You call.

River

The river is 9♠-6♥-5♠-3♥-Q♥. You hold 10♣-9♣.

There is $240 in the pot and it is $30 to bet.

Question 9. Do you (a) check (b) bet?

(a) ☐   (b) ☐   Points: ....

You check and John also checks. You show down your pair of 9s and it takes the pot. The hand history shows that John also had a pair of nines with 9♦-8♦ and you have out-kicked him.

Question 10. How would you rate John's play in this hand (a) poor (b) reasonable (c) good (d) very good?

(a) ☐   (b) ☐   (c) ☐   (d) ☐   Points: ....

                                           Total: ....

♣ — ♥ — ♦ — ♠ — ♣ — ♥ — ♦ — ♠

SCORECHART

100   Excellent. You valued your hand accurately and took the right steps to protect it.

90-99   Very good. Combating a player like John is not easy.

80-89   Good. Protecting a made hand is an important tactic in hold'em, and straightforward betting is not always the best way to achieve this.

70-79   Average. You may have pushed too hard or not hard enough.

60-69   Never mind. These modest made hands are difficult to handle.

below 60 Poor.

♣ — ♥ — ♦ — ♠ — ♣ — ♥ — ♦ — ♠

ANSWERS AND ANALYSIS

Holding: 10♣-9♣.

Question 1. (a) 0 (b) 2 (c) 5

This is a good hand with which to raise, even with bad position. If a king or queen comes on the flop you are in business, and if an ace comes you can bet and, if anyone shows interest, get away from the hand easily. It also prevents George from having a free flop.

Question 2. (a) 0 (b) 5 (c) 1

You have a decent drawing hand but nothing more, and are stuck with bad position for the whole hand. It can sometimes be worth raising with such a hand, but the circumstances need to be quite different. You need to be in late position, preferably the button, and you need one or two more callers. Note that, with a drawing hand, you are not worried about George getting a free flop.

Flop: 9♠-6♥-5♠. You hold 10♣-9♣.

Question 3. (a) 0 (b) 15 (c) 8

Question 4. (a) 0 (b) 4 (c) 15

You must think about what you are trying to achieve. You have a decent made hand which may or may not be winning. The priority now is to protect your hand in case it is winning. The way to protect your hand is to make sure that players with poor drawing hands are not getting the right odds to call. A poor drawing hand would be something like K-Q or 5-4, which are six and five outs respectively.

When there is $120 in the pot then such hands have an easy call if you bet out. It may be that John, on the button, decides to raise when it gets round to him. However, this will not help as the poor drawing hands still have the correct odds to call this raise. Therefore a better play is to check, in the anticipation that it will be checked around to John who, as the pre-flop raiser, then bets. You can then raise and confront David and George with a double bet if they want to play. By this time there will be $165 in the pot and it will be $30 for them to call. If they have weak drawing hands then they don't have the right odds and should fold. Note that they would also be afraid that they might get whiplashed, i.e. if they call they may face a further raise from John.

With just $60 in the pot the situation is entirely different. Now you can just bet out and any weak drawing hands already don't have the right price to play. Again, if they are contemplating a call, they have to fear a potential raise from John. You can try for a check-raise with the smaller pot, but it seems a little over the top and, because nobody raised pre-flop, there is a danger the pot might be checked around. Betting out is a far superior play.

Question 5. (a) 0 (b) 5 (c) 2

Three-betting is not terrible here, but there are many drawing possibilities on the flop, and I would prefer to see what the turn brings. There are a great many ugly cards that could turn up: any spade, 7, 8 or ace would be bad news. Even a 5 or a 6 or random overcards will leave you unsure as to whether your opponent has improved. Note that you also need to bear in mind that John may also hold a 9 in which case it is likely he has a better kicker than you. A-9, K-9, Q-9 and J-9 are all reasonable limping hands from the button (especially suited).

Turn: 9♠-6♥-5♠-3♥. You hold 10♣-9♣.

Question 6. (a) 3 (b) 10

The turn card is pleasantly blank and you should make the most of this with a bet. If John was drawing then his hand has not been helped. Let's see how he responds to a bet now. We have a good hand and don't want to give a free card with so many drawing possibilities.

Question 7. (a) 15 (b) 5 (c) 0

If you get raised here by a weak, passive player the game is pretty much up and it is hard to justify continuing. There are a number of perfectly plausible hands that Ben can hold against which you have insufficient outs to continue, e.g. 5-5, 6-6, 5-6, 7-8, A-9, K-9. Ben is not the kind of player to try his luck with a semi-bluff raise here.

Question 8. (a) 6 (b) 15 (c) 2

Getting raised here by a strong, aggressive player is rather different. It is quite possible that you are losing, but it could also be that John has a mediocre made hand with good drawing possibilities, for example a low pair and flush draw. You have 7-to-1 pot odds, and there should be sufficient doubt in your mind about John's hand that a call is worthwhile. If you choose to three-bet here then I salute your aggression, but don't ask me to back you in a game.

River: 9♠-6♥-5♠-3♥-Q♥. You hold 10♣-9♣.

Question 9. (a) 5 (b) 2

If you now bet, having already seen your flop and turn bets met by raises, then I admire your nerve. If you get raised again you will probably feel obliged to call and the hand will have cost you more money than it should. Checking (and calling if necessary) is a better play.

Question 10. (a) 0 (b) 0 (c) 5 (d) 10

John played this hand excellently. His raise on the turn put you under a lot of pressure and did not really cost him anything as he had enough of a hand to call you down anyway.

♣ — ♥ — ♦ — ♠ — ♣ — ♥ — ♦ — ♠

TIP: There are many factors to weigh up when trying to protect your hand: the pot size, your position and where the strong hand(s) are all need to be considered. Betting out is not always best and trying for a check-raise is not always best. Think about what you are trying to do and how best to achieve it.

Hand 9

Playing the Man

♣ — ♥ — ♦ — ♠ — ♣ — ♥ — ♦ — ♠

INTRODUCTION

This is a ten-player $20-$40 game. You are in the big blind with 5♣-5♠. TheMan is in the cut-off. TheMan is a very good player: tight, aggressive, combative and hard to read.

THE PLAY

Pre-flop

TheMan open-raises. The button and small blind both fold.

Hypothetical Play 1

TheMan is not in the cut-off but is UTG. He open-raises and the next eight players all fold. There is $70 in the pot and it is $20 to you.

Question 1. Do you (a) fold (b) call (c) raise?

(a) ☐	(b) ☐	(c) ☐	Points: ....

Hypothetical Play 2

Imagine that instead of the TheMan, you are facing Pussycat who *is* in the cut-off. Pussycat is a soft, weak and predictable player. It is folded round to Pussycat and Pussycat open-raises. The button and small blind fold. There is $70 in the pot and it is $20 to you.

Question 2. Do you (a) fold (b) call (c) raise?

(a) ☐	(b) ☐	(c) ☐	Points: ....

Actual Play

We are back now with the very good player TheMan – in the cut-off. There is $70 in the pot and it is $20 to you.

Question 3. Do you (a) fold (b) call (c) raise?

(a) ☐	(b) ☐	(c) ☐	Points: ....

You call.

Flop

The flop is J♥-6♠-3♣. You hold 5♣-5♠.

Hypothetical Play

Let's do ourselves a favour and get rid of TheMan again for a moment – he is hard work after all. Let's fight it out with Pussycat, who is an easier proposition. Assuming you just called the pre-flop raise, there is $90 in the pot and it is $20 to bet. There are many possible ways to play this hand. It is a reasonable assumption that if you now check, then your opponent will almost certainly bet. With this in mind...

Question 4. Do you (a) check, intending to fold (b) check, intending to call (c) check, intending to check-raise (d) bet?

(a) ☐	(b) ☐	(c) ☐	(d) ☐	Points: ....

Actual Play

We are now back with TheMan. There is $90 in the pot and it is $20 to bet. We can make the same assumption that if you now check, then your opponent will almost certainly bet. So...

Question 5. Do you (a) check, intending to fold (b) check, intending to call (c) check, intending to check-raise (d) bet?

(a) ☐	(b) ☐	(c) ☐	(d) ☐	Points: ....

You check and TheMan bets. You just call.

Turn

Hypothetical Turn

The turn is J♥-6♠-3♣-A♥. You hold 5♣-5♠.

There is $130 in the pot and it is $40 to bet.

Question 6. Do you (a) check, intending to fold (b) check, intending to call (c) check, intending to check-raise (d) bet?

(a) ☐   (b) ☐   (c) ☐   (d) ☐   Points: ....

Actual Turn

The turn is J♥-6♠-3♣-2♥. You hold 5♣-5♠.

There is $130 in the pot and it is $40 to bet.

Question 7. Do you (a) check, intending to fold (b) check, intending to call (c) check, intending to check-raise (d) bet?

(a) ☐   (b) ☐   (c) ☐   (d) ☐   Points: ....

You bet.

Hypothetical Play

TheMan now raises. There is $250 in the pot and it is $40 to you.

Question 8. Do you (a) fold (b) call (c) raise?

(a) ☐   (b) ☐   (c) ☐   Points: ....

Actual Play

TheMan just calls.

River

The river is J♥-6♠-3♣-2♥-J♦. You hold 5♣-5♠.

There is $210 in the pot and it is $40 to you.

Question 9. Do you (a) check (b) bet

(a) ☐   (b) ☐   Points: ....

Total: ....

You bet. TheMan thinks for a while and folds.

♣ — ♥ — ♦ — ♠ — ♣ — ♥ — ♦ — ♠

SCORECHART

100	Outstanding. You handled TheMan very well. Steve McQueen would have been impressed.
90-99	Excellent. There were many difficult decisions here.
80-89	Good, but you may have missed chances to take the initiative – and this can be fatal in poker.
70-79	Average.
60-69	Don't despair. These heads-up clashes are complex affairs.
below 60	Poor.

♣ — ♥ — ♦ — ♠ — ♣ — ♥ — ♦ — ♠

ANSWERS AND ANALYSIS

Holding: 5♣-5♠.

Question 1. (a) 5 (b) 2 (c) 0

Calling is not terrible but, as TheMan open-raised UTG, there is a great danger that your hand is dominated by a higher pair. Even if TheMan is opening with 'just' two high cards, then it is going to be difficult for you to play the hand successfully any time an ace, king, queen, or jack flops. Imagine the flop is K-9-2. He might be playing A-K and he might be playing A-Q – are you really going to pay $100 to go to the river and find out? If you could play perfect poker post-flop, then there might be some advantage to playing this hand. However, for mortal players, even good ones, the risk of making mistakes is too great, and it is better to just fold.

Question 2. (a) 0 (b) 7 (c) 10

Folding is absurd – you probably have the best hand right now. There is not much wrong with calling and seeing the flop but, against a weak player like Pussycat, I prefer to take the initiative with a raise. This often makes it easier to find out where you stand later on in the hand. Thus if the flop comes A-9-3 and you now bet and get called (or even raised), you can fairly safely assume you are beaten and get away from the hand cheaply.

If, alternatively, you simply called pre-flop, checked the flop and now Pussycat bets, you don't really know where you are. Is he betting an ace, a 9, K-Q, a pair of 2s? You just don't know and, consequently, it isn't clear how you should respond. You can't start thumping the pot when you could be playing just two outs but, on the other hand, you don't want to muck when you may be winning and it may be him who has just a few outs. From your point of view, it is a bit of a mess. It is much better to lead out and then reconsider the situation if you get some heat.

Another reason to take the initiative is that the player who is in the driving seat is usually the one who takes the pot when neither side has much. Let's suppose Pussycat is beating you with 7-7. You three-bet pre-flop, he calls, and now the flop comes A-K-Q. It is an appalling flop for you, but you bet anyway and – lo and behold – you probably get the goodies right away, even though you are playing a two-outer. Look what happens when you just call pre-flop and A-K-Q lands on the board – are you really going to bet? Of course not. You will check, Pussycat will bet and now you have to fold. The meek may inherit the earth, but they won't win much at the poker table.

Question 3. (a) 0 (b) 10 (c) 5

Out of position and up against a very good player, I prefer to see the flop cheaply here. A very good player is not going to be impressed by a three-bet, and may well just cap the pot, almost regardless of their holding. You should raise against Pussycat because it is easy to take the initiative away from the weakies. Tough players are a different proposition. They do not crawl into their shell as soon as they are raised (or re-raised), especially early on in the pot, so there is less to be gained by so doing.

Note that this situation is very different to that in Question 1. When The-Man is UTG, you can be pretty sure he has a powerful holding. When he is in the cut-off, he will be open-raising with a wide variety of hands – some strong, some not so strong. Your 5-5 is very playable here.

Flop: J♥-6♠-3♣. You hold 5♣-5♠.

Question 4. (a) 0 (b) 3 (c) 10 (d) 15

Note that in this particular scenario we have made a sub-optimal play pre-flop by failing to three-bet after Pussycat's raise. The best way to regain the initiative here is by betting out. Folding should be out of the question (for the moment anyway) and check-calling is feeble. Going for a check-raise is not a bad play, but it is a little over the top considering your modest holding. Bet out and see what he does.

Question 5. (a) 0 (b) 10 (c) 7 (d) 8

This is a very close decision, and what works well one day might well fail another.

Check-raising again seems over-aggressive for your modest holding. Suppose you check-raise and TheMan calls. What do you then do if a high card (ace, king or queen) comes on the turn? You will obliged to bet out, but it will then be horrible if you get raised.

Betting out cannot be bad, but I suspect TheMan will raise with pretty much any playable hand, or maybe even just call to trap you if he has a good hand, say K-J.

Check-calling is often horrible play in hold'em (or indeed any form of poker), but there is something to be said for it here. You get to see the turn card cheaply and can then decide what to do. It is much easier to judge where you think you are in the hand when you can see four board cards rather than just three.

Question 6. (a) 10 (b) 4 (c) 0 (d) 4

I know it is wimpy play, but it is likely that you are beaten here, and it is probably best to give up. Now and again you will be folding the winning hand, but there is nothing you can do about it – the percentage play is to fold. Poker is a game of imperfect information, and sometimes you just have to accept the fact that folding is the best play, even though there is a small chance you hold the best hand.

Turn: J♥-6♠-3♣-2♥. You hold 5♣-5♠.

Question 7. (a) 0 (b) 5 (c) 10 (d) 25

The turn card is a good one for you, giving you an extra four outs to a straight if you need them. It is time to take the initiative. If you check now, TheMan may well take a free card, and it will be galling if he out-draws you by pairing high.

Question 8. (a) 8 (b) 10 (c) 2

This is a tough decision because, if you call and the river is a blank, you will be obliged to call a further bet. This will cost you $80 in an attempt to win $290, assuming TheMan bets the river. However, the combination of your six outs, plus the decent chance that TheMan is bluffing or semi-bluffing, makes calling a preferable play to giving up. Furthermore, it is not great for your table image if you just cave in whenever you get popped on the turn. It is important to send a message that you cannot easily be pushed out of pots.

River: J♥-6♠-3♣-2♥-J♦. You hold 5♣-5♠.

Question 9. (a) 1 (b) 5

The J♦ is unlikely to have helped TheMan. If he had a jack in his hand you would probably have heard about it on the turn. It is probable that you are winning, and it is also likely that if you check TheMan will just check it back. Bet and hope for a crying call from two high cards.

Playing a mediocre hand, heads-up, out of position against a strong player is about as hard as it gets at hold'em. If you navigated your way through this hand successfully, you can be very pleased with yourself.

♣ — ♥ — ♦ — ♠ — ♣ — ♥ — ♦ — ♠

 TIP: With a modest holding which you have mentally decided you are taking to the river, it is easy to slip into check-call mode. Guard against this. Sometimes the turn card is helpful to you and very likely unhelpful to the opponent. When these situations arise, be prepared to take the initiative with a bet. Don't allow them the possibility of a free card.

Hand 10

Junk Shop

♣ — ♥ — ♦ — ♠ — ♣ — ♥ — ♦ — ♠

INTRODUCTION

This is a ten-player $15-$30 game. You are in the small blind with
Q♣-6♠. This is a new game for you, and you are not particularly familiar
with any of the players. However, you have been playing for a while and
it seems to be a good game. The players tend to be too loose pre-flop and,
post-flop, are calling along quite happily with all sorts of feeble holdings.
Most contested pots are taken down by hands like 9-7 offsuit. The big
blind is Cyclops. You have had a couple of tussles with Cyclops and have
noticed that he is basically self-obsessed. He only has eyes for his own
cards and only has ears for his own voice (and bets). Not much fun if you
are stuck next to him at a dinner party, but great to have in a poker
game, since he apparently remains blissfully unaware of the action
around him.

THE PLAY

Pre-flop

The UTG player limps, as do two middle players and the button. There is
$85 in the pot and it is $5 to you.

Hypothetical Play

The play is exactly the same, but your holding is 7♠-2♣.

Question 1. Do you (a) fold (b) call (c) raise?

(a) ☐   (b) ☐   (c) ☐   Points: ....

Actual Play

We now reconstruct your marvellous holding of Q♣-6♠.

Question 2. Do you (a) fold (b) call (c) raise?

(a) ☐   (b) ☐   (c) ☐   Points: ....

You call.

Cyclops now ponders a while and, to your dismay, raises. Entirely predictable, the next four players all call quickly. There is $165 in the pot and it is $15 to you.

Hypothetical Play

I am now going to whip away your fine Q♣-6♠ and replace it with 7♠-2♣.

Question 3. Do you (a) fold (b) call (c) raise?

(a) ☐   (b) ☐   (c) ☐   Points: ....

Actual Play

Okay, you can have your Q♣-6♠ back now.

Question 4. Do you (a) fold (b) call (c) raise?

(a) ☐   (b) ☐   (c) ☐   Points: ....

You decide to call.

Flop

The flop comes down Q♥-Q♣-4♥. You hold Q♣-6♠.

There is $180 in the pot and it is $15 to you.

Question 5. Let's assume you are not likely to fold right away here. There are various ways you could try to play this hand, but which of the following do you prefer (a) check, planning a check-raise (b) bet?

(a) ☐   (b) ☐   Points: ....

You check. Much to your surprise Cyclops now checks immediately. The other four players all ponder but, eventually, they all check too.

Turn

The turn is Q♥-Q♣-4♥-3♦. You hold Q♣-6♠.

There is $180 in the pot and it is $30 to you.

Question 6. Do you (a) check, planning a check-raise (b) bet?

(a) ☐	(b) ☐	Points: ....

You bet. Cyclops now leaps into action with an instant raise. The next two players fold, but then the late middle player MrSoftee, of whom you know next to nothing other than that he seems rather feeble, calls. There is $330 in the pot and it is $30 to you.

Question 7. Do you (a) fold (b) call (c) raise?

(a) ☐	(b) ☐	(c) ☐	Points: ....

You raise. Cyclops, barely pausing for breath, now caps the betting, and MrSoftee calls. There is $510 in the pot and it is $30 to you.

Question 8. Do you (a) fold (b) call?

(a) ☐	(b) ☐	Points: ....

You call.

River

Hypothetical River

The river is Q♥-Q♣-4♥-3♦-6♥. You hold Q♣-6♠.

There is $540 in the pot and it is $30 to bet.

Question 9. Do you (a) check (b) bet?

(a) ☐	(b) ☐	Points: ....

Actual River

The river is Q♥-Q♣-4♥-3♦-9♥. You hold Q♣-6♠.

There is $540 in the pot and it is $30 to bet.

Question 10. Do you (a) check (b) bet?

(a) ☐	(b) ☐		Points: ....

You check. Slightly surprisingly, Cyclops checks. MrSoftee also fails to disturb the pot. MrSoftee shows 8♥-5♥ and takes the pot with his weedy flush. Cyclops had A♥-A♣.

Question 11. Did MrSoftee make a mistake by not betting the river (a) absolutely (b) yes, but it was a tricky decision (c) no?

(a) ☐	(b) ☐	(c) ☐	Points: ....
			Total: ....

♣ — ♥ — ♦ — ♠ — ♣ — ♥ — ♦ — ♠

SCORECHART

100   Excellent. You handled your junk very well, which is never easy at hold'em.

90-99   Very good. Anyone would think you played junk cards all the time!

80-89   Good. You probably missed the turn re-raise. Concentrate on what you know about the opposition.

70-79   Average.

60-69   The bad news is: you need more practice with junk. The good news is: you will get a ton of it during your hold'em career.

below 60 Poor.

♣ — ♥ — ♦ — ♠ — ♣ — ♥ — ♦ — ♠

ANSWERS AND ANALYSIS

Holding: Q♣-6♠.

Question 1. (a) 3 (b) 5 (c) 0

The bad news is that you are in the worst possible position and your hand is as bad as it gets. The good news is that you are getting 17-to-1 pot odds. With 17-to-1 pot odds, I would play anything but, even so, it is difficult to believe that folding is that much of an error.

Question 2. (a) 1 (b) 5 (c) 0

The same 17-to-1 pot odds are still enticing you in, and now you even have a picture card. This is a clear call, but please remember that you need to play the hand well, i.e. know when to dump it.

Question 3. (a) 5 (b) 0 (c) 0

This raise is horrible for you but, hey, you only lost five dollars. It is unlikely that Cyclops would raise without a big pair, so you will have to make some highly improbable hand in order to win. It was just about worth calling before as no-one had announced any sort of holding and you had 17-to-1 pot odds. Also it only cost you $5. Now Cyclops is telling the world that he has a biggie, you only have 11-to-1 pot odds and it is going to cost you $15. This is your stop. Out please.

Question 4. (a) 5 (b) 2 (c) 0

Folding is still correct here. All the arguments from Question 3 remain valid and, in view of the fact that Cyclops has a decent hand, your Q♣-6♠ is barely more enticing than 2♣-7♠. The best realistic result is a queen-high flop and even then you may still be losing to Cyclops or be out-kicked by one of your other four opponents. Junk hands are just that – junk.

If you chose to raise as an answer to any of the Questions 1-4, then I suggest you stick to the $0.50/$1 games for the foreseeable future.

Flop: Q♥-Q♣-4♥. You hold Q♣-6♠.

Question 5. (a) 7 (b) 10

There are a number of imponderables in this hand, and it is difficult to know what will work out best. There are two key issues here. If you are losing, this is a bad trap hand and you are probably playing three outs. It will be hard to dump the hand but, if you are trapped, you don't want to lose any more money than necessary. If you are winning, you want to make any flush draws pay heavily to try and draw out on you. It is not easy to pursue these joint aims simultaneously.

If you bet then, knowing Cyclops, he will probably raise. This will confront your other four opponents with a double bet, and then even these sheep will probably fold unless they have a queen or a flush draw. If you check, Cyclops will probably bet, and if there is then action (or even just calling) from the others, it will be hard to know where you stand. A bet, which will probably force four other opponents to pay a double bet, is more likely to clarify the situation.

Finally, there is a small possibility that the hand may be checked round. This would be a horrible time to give a free card, since there is a two-flush on the board.

Turn: Q♥-Q♣-4♥-3♦. You hold Q♣-6♠.

Question 6. (a) 3 (b) 10

Your check has rebounded badly on you and you cannot keep quiet any longer. Cyclops' instant check on the flop is mysterious, but maybe he was also hoping to check-raise. Bet now and find out what is going on. If you check again now, you will still not have a clue what is happening.

Question 7. (a) 0 (b) 15 (c) 25

You have to consider what your opponents have here. Does anyone have a hand that can be beating yours? Cyclops probably does not have a queen, as he raised pre-flop, out of position and most likely has a big pair. It is unlikely that MrSoftee has a queen. If he did it would be very strange play to check the flop. It smells very much like he has a draw – most likely a flush draw, although 6-5 is possible. On the balance of probabilities, you likely have the best hand and should raise.

Question 8. (a) 0 (b) 5

You have to be slightly less happy about your hand now, but folding would be insane.

Question 9. (a) 10 (b) 5

There is a God after all. You now hold the absolute nuts. Not only that, but a flush draw will have got there. Checking is definitely the best play here. Cyclops may well bet and ... you never know ... he might even get raised by MrSoftee. You could pick up a stack of bets on the river. You could bet, but then even Cyclops will probably spot the three-flush and only call. It is unlikely that MrSoftee, even with a flush, will then raise.

River: Q♥-Q♣-4♥-3♦-9♥. You hold Q♣-6♠.

Question 10. (a) 10 (b) 2

The river is horrible for you. It looks like MrSoftee has made a flush. Sometimes in situations such as this you can bet and fold if you are raised. However, the pot is now so big that you will be obliged to call any river bets, so it is best to try and keep it cheap.

Question 11. (a) 10 (b) 1 (c) 0

MrSoftee's check is horrible. Obviously he is worried that his flush is so miniscule that someone may have a bigger one. Or maybe he is worried that someone is sandbagging with a full house. Neither scenario is remotely likely, and his check cost him two big bets, as you would have had to call, and it would be quite out of character for Cyclops to dump his pocket aces here. It is especially poor bearing in mind that there was no betting on the river, and thus the likelihood of his flush being good was very high.

♣ — ♥ — ♦ — ♠ — ♣ — ♥ — ♦ — ♠

TIP: You have to know your opponents. When you get raised on the turn, it is tempting to just slip into check-call mode. However, at that point you may still have the best hand, and there may not be that many outs against you. If you think about your opponents you will often conclude that, on the balance of probabilities, you have the best hand and a raise is in order.

Hand 11

Porkies

♣ — ♥ — ♦ — ♠ — ♣ — ♥ — ♦ — ♠

INTRODUCTION

This is a ten-player $20-$40 game. You are sitting in the big blind with K♣-J♥. The UTG (first to act after the blinds) is Vienna. You don't know much about him, but he seems to be a reasonable player. The small blind is Porkie. Porkie is pretty loose pre-flop. Post-flop he is an unconventional but by no means bad player.

THE PLAY

Pre-flop

Hypothetical Pre-flop

Vienna opens with a raise and it is passed around to Porkie, who calls. There is $100 in the pot. It is $20 to you.

Question 1. Do you: (a) fold (b) call (c) raise?

(a) ☐	(b) ☐	(c) ☐	Points: ....

Actual Pre-flop

Vienna limps and it is passed around to Porkie, who raises. There is $80 in the pot. It is $20 to you.

Question 2. Do you: (a) fold (b) call (c) raise?

(a) ☐	(b) ☐	(c) ☐	Points: ....

You call and Vienna also calls. The pot is now $120.

Flop

The flop is a nice one for you: J♣-9♦-3♦. You hold K♣-J♥.

Porkie now bets. There is $140 in the pot and it is $20 to you.

Question 3. Do you: (a) fold (b) call (c) raise?

(a) ☐	(b) ☐	(c) ☐	Points: ....

You raise.

Hypothetical Play

Vienna now three-bets and Porkie caps the betting. There is $300 in the pot and it is $40 to you.

Question 4. Do you: (a) fold (b) call?

(a) ☐	(b) ☐	Points: ....

Actual Play

You raise, Vienna folds and Porkie just calls. There is $200 in the pot.

Turn

The turn is J♣-9♦-3♦-5♣. You hold K♣-J♥.

Slightly to your surprise, Porkie now bets – a typically confusing Porkie move. There is $240 in the pot and it is $40 to you.

Question 5. Do you: (a) fold (b) call (c) raise?

(a) ☐	(b) ☐	(c) ☐	Points: ....

You raise and Porkie just calls.

River

Hypothetical River

The river is J♣-9♦-3♦-5♣-5♦. You hold K♣-J♥.

Porkie checks. There is $360 in the pot.

Question 6. Do you: (a) check (b) bet?

(a) ☐	(b) ☐	Points: ....

Actual River

The river is J♣-9♦-3♦-5♣-8♣. You hold K♣-J♥.

Porkie checks. There is $360 in the pot.

Question 7. Do you: (a) check (b) bet?

(a) ☐	(b) ☐	Points: ....

You bet and Porkie now check-raises. There is $480 in the pot and it is $40 to you.

Question 8. Do you: (a) fold (b) call (c) raise?

(a) ☐	(b) ☐	(c) ☐	Points: ....
			Total: ....

You call and Porkie shows you A♣-9♣ for a backdoor flush.

♣ — ♥ — ♦ — ♠ — ♣ — ♥ — ♦ — ♠

SCORECHART

100   Excellent. You have a good feel for when to push your hands and when to ease off.

90-99   Very good.

80-89   Good. You may need to concentrate more on the texture of the board.

70-79   Average.

60-69   You have probably overestimated/underestimated your holding at various points.

below 60   Poor.

♣ — ♥ — ♦ — ♠ — ♣ — ♥ — ♦ — ♠

ANSWERS AND ANALYSIS

Holding: K♣-J♥.

Question 1. (a) 10 (b) 6 (c) 0

When a decent player open-raises UTG in a full ring game you need a very decent hand to compete. You are getting 5-to-1 for your $20, but it is still best to fold. The trouble is that your hand is very likely to be domi-

nated by Vienna. If you consider the hands Vienna is likely to hold, you
will see that virtually all of them leave you dominated, e.g. A-K, A-J, K-
Q, Q-Q, J-J all leave you trying to hit one card, while A-A and K-K are
even worse news. If you are going to play you have to hope that Vienna
has A-Q or a pair lower than jacks, and that you hit on the flop. Even
then, you still have to worry about Porkie. K-J is just not good enough
here. If you do happen to win with it you are unlikely to get paid much,
whereas if you make some sort of hand and end up losing (a serious possibility since it is likely you are dominated) it will be expensive.

Question 2. (a) 7 (b) 10 (c) 2

You have a moderate hand but, assuming that Vienna will call, you are
getting 5-to-1 for your $20. This is a decent call and folding would be
rather limp. On the other hand, raising would be way over the top. Vienna, who is a decent player, has position on you and may well have you
dominated with A-J or K-Q – typical limping hands for a good player
UTG. Porkie has already raised out of position, suggesting a decent holding – although knowing Porkie it is also possible he has a feeble hand.
Nevertheless, why not just see the flop without escalating the pot?

Flop: J♣-9♦-3♦. You hold K♣-J♥.

Question 3. (a) 0 (b) 2 (c) 10

You have top pair, excellent kicker. Anything other than a raise here is
very weak. Some players might like to just call here, planning to raise the
turn, but this is poor play as it allows Vienna to compete with all sorts of
hands. It is much harder for Vienna to have a hand that can sensibly call
a double bet.

Question 4. (a) 10 (b) 2

War has broken out, and what once looked like a good holding now seems
decidedly feeble. Vienna and Porkie are both sensible players, and you
must be beaten here. It is possible one player is on a diamond draw, but
the other almost certainly has a better hand with a set, an overpair, J-9
or A-J or a set. You are getting 7½-to-1 for your money and have, at most,
five outs. A further problem is that two of your improving cards – K♦ and
J♦ – both put a three-flush on board. This is a clear fold.

Turn: J♣-9♦-3♦-5♣. You hold K♣-J♥.

Question 5. (a) 2 (b) 10 (c) 20

Why is Porkie suddenly betting when he only called your raise on the
flop? If he had a monster hand, surely he would have three-bet the flop?
The likely explanation is that Porkie has a decent holding which he sus-
pects is probably winning, and does not want to give you a free card. He

can see that if you were on a flush or straight draw, you have missed. It is also quite possible that he has now picked up a flush draw himself and is using it to apply pressure.

In either case, your hand is very probably better than Porkie thinks it is, and a raise is in order.

Question 6. (a) 2 (b) 10

The 5♦ creates a pair and a three-flush but, nevertheless, is not really that scary. Although Porkie bet the turn, it is most improbable that he has a 5 in his hand. It is also unlikely that he is on a diamond flush draw. If that was the case the more natural aggressive play would be to three-bet the flop, rather than suddenly bet out on the turn.

River: J♣-9♦-3♦-5♣-8♣. You hold K♣-J♥.

Question 7. (a) 25 (b) 10

The 8♣ is an ugly card. There are many hands that Porkie could hold that have now improved to beat you. A club flush draw has made it, as has an open-ended straight draw with Q-10. Also, as Porkie is fairly loose pre-flop, J-8 and 9-8 as holdings are not out of the question. Checking and showing down is in order. Betting and being raised will be no fun at all. The pot is now big enough that you will feel very inclined to call but you will almost certainly be beat.

Question 8. (a) 4 (b) 5 (c) 0

This has all gone pear-shaped. Well, you have to call really, but don't hold your breath. You are getting 12-to-1 for your money, and once in a while you will catch Porkie bluffing.

♣ — ♥ — ♦ — ♠ — ♣ — ♥ — ♦ — ♠

 TIP: When you suspect an opponent is on a drawing hand, you must carefully consider their possible holdings and think about whether the turn and river cards are likely to have been helpful to them.

Hand 12

Gone Fishing

♣ — ♥ — ♦ — ♠ — ♣ — ♥ — ♦ — ♠

INTRODUCTION

This is a seven-player $15-$30 game. You are in the big blind with A♣-K♠. You are not particularly familiar with the players, but the game is rather passive with most of the opposition playing fairly loosely and calling along with mediocre hands. No-one, apart from you of course, is doing much raising. It is a good game in which to play. Heatwave and Munster seem typical of the players on this table.

THE PLAY

Pre-flop

Heatwave is UTG and limps. It is passed around to Munster in the small blind, who chucks $5 into the pot. There is $45 in the pot. You can check or raise.

Hypothetical Play 1

Assume you have K♠-Q♥.

Question 1. Do you (a) check (b) raise?

(a) ☐   (b) ☐   Points: ....

Hypothetical Play 2

Assume you have Q♠-J♥.

Question 2. Do you (a) check (b) raise?

(a) ☐   (b) ☐   Points: ....

Hypothetical Play 3

Assume you have J♠-10♥.

Question 3. Do you (a) check (b) raise?

(a) ☐	(b) ☐		Points: ....

Actual Play

Enough of the imaginary play. You hold A♣-K♠.

Question 4. Do you (a) check (b) raise?

(a) ☐	(b) ☐		Points: ....

You raise. Both Heatwave and Munster call.

Flop

Hypothetical Flop

The flop is 10♦-9♠-8♦. You hold A♣-K♠.

Munster checks. There is $90 in the pot and it is $15 to bet.

Question 5. Do you (a) check (b) bet?

(a) ☐	(b) ☐		Points: ....

Actual Flop

The flop is 10♦-6♠-3♦. You hold A♣-K♠.

Munster checks. There is $90 in the pot and it is $15 to bet.

Question 6. Do you (a) check (b) bet?

You bet and both opponents call.

(a) ☐	(b) ☐		Points: ....

Turn

Hypothetical Turn 1

The turn is 10♦-6♠-3♦-Q♠. You hold A♣-K♠.

Munster checks. There is $135 in the pot and it is $30 to bet.

Question 7. Do you (a) check (b) bet?

(a) ☐   (b) ☐   Points: ....

Hypothetical Turn 2

The turn is 10♦-6♠-3♦-8♠. You hold A♣-K♠.

Munster checks. There is $135 in the pot and it is $30 to bet.

Question 8. Do you (a) check (b) bet?

(a) ☐   (b) ☐   Points: ....

Actual Turn

The turn is 10♦-6♠-3♦-3♣. You hold A♣-K♠.

Munster checks. There is $135 in the pot and it is $30 to bet.

Question 9. Do you (a) check (b) bet?

(a) ☐   (b) ☐   Points: ....

You bet, Heatwave calls but Munster folds.

River

The river is 10♦-6♠-3♦-3♣-2♣. You hold A♣-K♠.

There is $195 in the pot and it is $30 to bet.

Question 10. Do you (a) check (b) bet?

(a) ☐   (b) ☐   Points: ....

You check and Heatwave now bets. There is $225 in the pot and it is $30 to you.

Question 11. Do you (a) fold (b) call (c) raise?

(a) ☐   (b) ☐   (c) ☐   Points: ....

You call. Heatwave shows 9♦-7♦ and you take down the pot with your ace-high.

Question 12. How would you rate Heatwave's play in this hand (a) good (b) mediocre (c) poor (d) very poor?

(a) ☐   (b) ☐   (c) ☐   (d) ☐   Points: ....

Total: ....

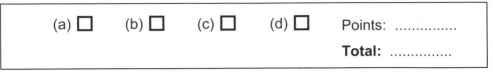

SCORECHART

100   Outstanding. Some questions were straightforward, but there were also a number of difficult decisions here.

90-99   Excellent. Not a lot passed you by.

80-89   Good. Overcards are never easy to play, and you got most things right.

70-79   You were probably either too aggressive or too passive. Overcard play is tricky; judge each situation on its merits.

60-69   Play through the hand again and take another look at Hand 2, which also features overcard play.

below 60   Poor.

ANSWERS AND ANALYSIS

Holding: A♣-K♠.

Question 1. (a) 1 (b) 5

It is quite likely that you have the best hand. These players, especially Munster in the small blind, will limp with any old rubbish, and you have a fairly decent holding. Make them pay to see the flop. If the flop is ragged with an ace you will bet, and you can easily release the hand if you get played with.

Question 2. (a) 2 (b) 5

Q♠-J♥ is quite a lot worse than K♠-Q♥. Nevertheless, these players are passive and may well pay you off if you hit top pair, especially in a raised pot.

Question 3. (a) 5 (b) 3

Your hand is now just too weak to justify a raise. You may even be losing to both opponents. There is also more chance of you now making a pair, but with an overcard also appearing on the flop. This will make the hand that much harder to play.

Question 4. (a) 0 (b) 5

This is about as close to a no-brainer as it gets. Players are sometimes loathe to raise with just high cards as you will so often miss the flop. However, your expectation in the pot exceeds that of your opponents and you *must* raise here.

Question 5. (a) 10 (b) 4

This is about as bad a flop as you could get for your hand against a couple of pre-flop limpers. Even though you should almost always be aggressive when you have raised pre-flop against a small field, it is not worth it here. A major reason to bet in a situation like this is that you might well take down the pot at once if no-one else has anything. However, the chance of neither player having connected at all with this flop is remote. These players will call at the slightest excuse, so if either of them holds a queen, jack, 10, 9, 8, 7 or even a 6, they are going to at least call.

Furthermore, since Munster has already checked, there is a reasonable chance that Heatwave may also check, and you will get to see the turn card for free. This would be good news and it would also give you a much better idea where you stand, and if you have any realistic chance to take down the pot.

Flop: 10♦-6♠-3♦. You hold A♣-K♠.

Question 6. (a) 2 (b) 10

Considering that the flop missed you, this is not too bad and you must bet here. There is a now a decent chance that both opponents will fold and that alone justifies betting. Even removing one opponent would be an achievement. Failing to bet here is very feeble.

Question 7. (a) 3 (b) 10

You have picked up a gutshot draw, so if someone has a pair you have up to ten possible outs, and this gives you the impetus you need to keep up the pressure. It is not very likely that the queen has made anyone else a big hand, so you probably won't have to face a raise. You certainly have enough of a hand to call a bet, so go ahead and bet yourself. You never know – they may both fold.

It is often said that it is better to bet hands with few outs and check hands with more outs. However, poker is a situational game and this advice doesn't apply here. If your opponents were tough, tricky players, who could raise you here with all sorts of holdings, then you might be inclined to check, as you would not want to be pushed off a hand where you could have up to ten outs. However, if you get raised by the passive players in this game then you should consider dumping your hand, as you possibly only have the four outs to the straight, and this doesn't justify continuing in the pot.

Your opponents have – true to form – both been completely passive to date. Such players often hang around with very moderate holdings on the cheap streets, but then think better of it when the bet size doubles. Bet your hand.

Question 8. (a) 10 (b) 3

This scenario is very much worse than that in Question 7, since the 8♠ does nothing for your hand but has probably helped one or other of your opponents. Anyone who was calling along with a gutshot to make a 10-high straight now has, at the very least, a pair and a gutshot draw, and is probably going to the river. A player with 10-9 or 7-6 has now also picked up a gutshot and essentially has the same hand. Check and hope for a free card.

Turn: 10♦-6♠-3♦-3♣. You hold A♣-K♠.

Question 9. (a) 4 (b) 10

It is unlikely that the 3♣ has helped anyone, so you must keep up the pressure.

River: 10♦-6♠-3♦-3♣-2♣. You hold A♣-K♠.

Question 10. (a) 10 (b) 0

There is no reason to bet. If you bet and get called there is almost no chance that you are winning. There is also no possibility that you will persuade Heatwave to lay down the winning hand. He is certainly going to call with any pair. There is a further advantage to checking as you give Heatwave the chance to bluff...

Question 11. (a) 0 (b) 10 (c) 2

You must call here. You only have to win one time in seven to show a profit and will certainly do that. Raising against Heatwave is pointless. He is not the kind of tough player who can fold a winning hand here.

Question 12. (a) 0 (b) 0 (c) 3 (d) 10

Heatwave's conduct of this hand was abysmal – he played badly on every street. Pre-flop UTG his 9♦-7♦ is unplayable, and he should certainly fold. The flop gave him at least 12 outs and he should have put you – and indeed Munster – under pressure with a raise. If he were to raise here and then bet the turn it would be hard for you to call him down with just A-K. Even on the turn a raise was a better play than calling. Again it will be very hard for you to call down with just your ace, and Munster will need something pretty big to call $60 cold. Finally, his river bluff was fairly hopeless. You raised pre-flop slightly out of position and bet every street. You are unlikely to give up now when his play has indicated strongly that he has a drawing hand and this appears to have missed.

♣ — ♥ — ♦ — ♠ — ♣ — ♥ — ♦ — ♠

TIP: Try to find games with weak players like Heatwave. A good player would have made life very difficult for you in this pot, whereas he just called along passively with his draw and then threw you an extra bet on the river for good measure when he missed.

Hand 13

Russian Roulette

♣ − ♥ − ♦ − ♠ − ♣ − ♥ − ♦ − ♠

INTRODUCTION

This is a ten-player $20-$40 game. You are in the cut-off seat with
A♣-J♠. The button is Dmitri, a reasonable player who lists his home
town as Moscow and is tight and very aggressive. His aggression makes
him tough to play against, but his weakness is that he can sometimes be
rather hot-headed and tends not to think too deeply. He also has a ten-
dency to focus too much on his own holding without considering what
other players might have. He occasionally goes on tilt and bets his hands
far too hard. If you want an image of Dmitri think of the John Malkovich
character Teddy KGB in the film *Rounders*.

THE PLAY

Pre-flop

It is passed around to you. There is $30 in the pot and it is $20 to you.

Question 1. Do you (a) fold (b) call (c) raise?

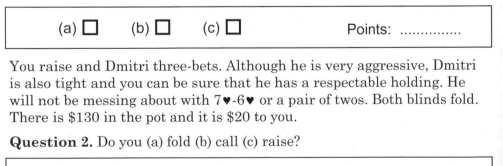

(a) ☐   (b) ☐   (c) ☐   Points: ....

You raise and Dmitri three-bets. Although he is very aggressive, Dmitri
is also tight and you can be sure that he has a respectable holding. He
will not be messing about with 7♥-6♥ or a pair of twos. Both blinds fold.
There is $130 in the pot and it is $20 to you.

Question 2. Do you (a) fold (b) call (c) raise?

(a) ☐   (b) ☐   (c) ☐   Points: ....

You call.

Flop

The flop is J♠-10♥-4♣. You hold A♣-J♠.

There is $150 in the pot and it is $20 to bet. Let's assume that, having made top pair, top kicker, you are not going to dump your hand just yet.

Question 3. Do you (a) check, planning a check-raise (b) bet?

(a) ☐   (b) ☐   Points: ....

You check, Dmitri bets and you raise. Dmitri thinks for a while and, slightly to your surprise, just calls.

Hypothetical Play

As with Question 3, but instead of just calling your check-raise, Dmitri now three-bets you fairly quickly. There is $250 in the pot and it is $20 to you.

Question 4. Do you (a) fold (b) call (c) cap the betting?

(a) ☐   (b) ☐   (c) ☐   Points: ....

Turn

The turn is J♠-10♥-4♣-9♥. You hold A♣-J♠. There is $230 in the pot and it is $40 to bet.

Question 5. Do you (a) check (b) bet?

(a) ☐   (b) ☐   Points: ....

You bet.

Hypothetical Play

Dmitri now raises you. There is $350 in the pot and it is $40 to you.

Question 6. Do you (a) fold (b) call (c) raise?

(a) ☐   (b) ☐   (c) ☐   Points: ....

Actual Play

Dmitri just calls.

River

The river is J♠-10♥-4♣-9♥-A♥. You hold A♣-J♠.

There is $310 in the pot and it is $40 to bet.

Question 7. Do you (a) check, hoping to check-raise (b) bet?

(a) ☐   (b) ☐   Points: ....

You bet and Dmitri now raises. There is $430 in the pot and it is $40 to you.

Question 8. Do you (a) fold (b) call (c) raise?

(a) ☐   (b) ☐   (c) ☐   Points: ....

                                          Total: ....

You raise and Dmitri calls. Your top two pair wins and the hand history shows that he had A♣-10♣ for a worse two pair. Your good, aggressive play is rewarded with a nice pot.

♣ — ♥ — ♦ — ♠ — ♣ — ♥ — ♦ — ♠

SCORECHART

100   Outstanding. Players like Dmitri will give you a lot of trouble and you handled him very well.

90-99   Excellent. There were many hard decisions here.

80-89   Very good. You must have got the river play right and that was tough.

70-79   You need to think more about what your opponent holds.

60-69   Never mind. This was a difficult hand. Good job it wasn't really Russian Roulette.

below 60   Poor.

♣ — ♥ — ♦ — ♠ — ♣ — ♥ — ♦ — ♠

ANSWERS AND ANALYSIS

Holding: A♣-J♠.

Question 1. (a) 0 (b) 0 (c) 5

You have more than enough of a hand to open-raise. You should make this play even from middle position or early position if the game is not too tight.

Question 2. (a) 0 (b) 5 (c) 1

Dmitri's raise is not good news. He is a reasonably tough player, he will have some sort of hand and he has position over you. You need to hit something on the flop.

Flop: J♠-10♥-4♣. You hold A♣-J♠.

Question 3. (a) 8 (b) 10

This is a very close decision, but I would be slightly more inclined to bet. It is quite likely that Dmitri has A-K or A-Q and, with such a holding, he will probably raise as, from his point of view, he is looking at either seven or ten outs. There is a very good chance that you have the best hand and then you can three-bet for value.

If you check-raise instead, then Dmitri may just call. You should take the view that you probably have the best hand, and should try to get as much money into the pot as you can. Betting out offers the best chance for this.

Question 4. (a) 0 (b) 5 (c) 10

We know that Dmitri is very aggressive and should not be too surprised at his three-bet. The flop is the cheap betting round, and players are very loose with their bets and raises. Until Dmitri demonstrates some serious strength on the turn you should assume you are ahead in this pot. There are many hands that you are beating that he would play hard on this flop, e.g. A-K, A-Q, A-10, K-Q and K-J. You are only behind against the big pairs, A-A through to 10-10 (you are also behind against J-10, but Dmitri would probably not three-bet pre-flop with such a mediocre holding) and the former collection are far more likely than the latter.

Turn: J♠-10♥-4♣-9♥. You hold A♣-J♠.

Question 5. (a) 0 (b) 5

The 9♥ is mildly scary, as the holding K-Q has now made a straight. However, you must bet here and see how Dmitri responds.

Question 6. (a) 2 (b) 15 (c) 0

It is time to switch into call-down mode. Of course if Dmitri has K-Q, J-J or 10-10 you have no outs at all, but we know that Dmitri is very aggressive, and he may well be semi-bluffing here, as the 9♥ creates various drawing possibilities with some of Dmitri's likely holdings. If he has A♥-K♥ or A♥-Q♥ he has picked up a flush draw and if he has some other flavour of A-Q he has picked up an extra four outs as an 8 now makes a straight. If he is playing K-K or Q-Q we still have five outs, and this is just about enough for a call on the pot odds. Dmitri's raise is undoubtedly bad news, but the pot is now too big to just give up. Dmitri may well be semi-bluffing and you have the best hand, or he may be playing an over-pair when you still have outs. Folding is definitely wrong here and raising is ridiculous.

River: J♠-10♥-4♣-9♥-A♥. You hold A♣-J♠.

Question 7. (a) 5 (b) 20

If you think about it, it is not likely that this card has given Dmitri a winning hand. The only plausible flush draw that has come in is K♥-Q♥, and if Dmitri had this, he would have made a straight on the turn and you would have heard about it. We know that Dmitri doesn't go over-board pre-flop, so he isn't playing small hearts or something ropey like K♥-8♥. You are also losing to A-A, but that requires Dmitri to have precisely the two missing aces, and again he might well have raised on the turn with this holding.

You have hit top two pair and you should bet. If you try for a check-raise, then Dmitri may become suspicious and just check it back, even with A-K or A-Q. Betting is good as you will probably get crying calls from hands like K-J and Q-J.

Question 8. (a) 0 (b) 10 (c) 30

Dmitri's raise is puzzling. We worked out, in the answer to Question 7, that the A♥ was very unlikely to give him a winning hand. So, you are probably only losing if he has slowplayed a hand like K♥-Q♥ or 10-10. However, this is not Dmitri's style. When he has a hand he bangs in the money on the turn. He doesn't mess about waiting until the river to get in his raise. Also, slowplaying these hands on the turn would be horrible play with so many possible draws out there.

It does not seem probable that Dmitri is making some hopeless bluff – it is more likely that he genuinely believes that the A♥ has made him a winning hand and he is raising for value. So what is his holding? Most likely he has made top pair with A-K or A-Q and has got carried away, as

Dmitri is wont to do. It is also possible that he has A-10 and made a worse two pair, and he may also be sharing the pot, holding A-J himself. Of the hands that Dmitri could have improved with on the river, you are only losing to A-A, and the other holdings identified above are much more likely. You should raise for value with your two pair.

♣ — ♥ — ♦ — ♠ — ♣ — ♥ — ♦ — ♠

 TIP: Accurate river play is an underestimated feature in hold'em. Players are too often relieved just to have made it to the river and are happy to show down their hands and see who gets the goods. Resist this temptation and focus on the specific situation. If you judge that (on the balance of probabilities) you have the best holding – and can get called by a weaker hand – then bet or raise for value.

Hand 14

Protection Racket

♣ – ♥ – ♦ – ♠ – ♣ – ♥ – ♦ – ♠

INTRODUCTION

This is a ten-player $20-$40 game. You are first to speak with K♣-K♠. This is a good game with typically four or five players seeing each flop. The majority of players are loose and passive and will pay off and chase with all sorts of mediocre holdings. Banjo and Gazza are middle position players who both happily fit the above description. HellRaiser is in the big blind, and he is just about the only decent player you have noticed at the table.

THE PLAY

Pre-flop

You are UTG. There is $30 in the pot and it is $20 to call.

Hypothetical Pre-flop 1

You are UTG with your black kings. The game is not as described above. Instead it is a rather tight, tough game. Most flops are taken three-handed or four at most and many are heads-up. There are only a couple of loose players. Let's assume you are not going to muck your pair of kings.

Question 1. Do you (a) call, hoping for a raise so you can three-bet (b) raise?

(a) ☐   (b) ☐   Points: ....

102

Hypothetical Pre-flop 2

The game is as described in Question 1, only now you are sitting in middle position and it is passed around to you.

Question 2. Do you (a) call, hoping for a raise so you can three-bet (b) raise?

(a) ☐   (b) ☐   Points: ....

Actual Pre-flop

Returning to the actual game with all the nice loose players.

Question 3. Do you (a) call, hoping for a raise so you can three-bet (b) raise?

(a) ☐   (b) ☐   Points: ....

You raise. Banjo and Gazza both call, as does HellRaiser.

Flop

The flop is Q♣-9♥-8♣. You hold K♣-K♠.

HellRaiser checks. There is $170 in the pot and it is $20 to bet.

Question 4. Do you (a) check, hoping to check-raise (b) bet?

(a) ☐   (b) ☐   Points: ....

You bet, and both Banjo and Gazza call fairly quickly. HellRaiser now check-raises you. There is $270 in the pot and it is $20 to you.

Question 5. Do you (a) fold (b) call (c) re-raise?

(a) ☐   (b) ☐   (c) ☐   Points: ....

You call. Banjo and Gazza also call.

Turn

Hypothetical Turn

The turn is Q♣-9♥-8♣-10♦. You hold K♣-K♠.

HellRaiser bets. There is $370 in the pot and it is $40 to you.

Question 6. Do you (a) fold (b) call (c) raise?

(a) ☐   (b) ☐   (c) ☐   Points: ....

Actual Turn

The turn is Q♣-9♥-8♣-4♦. You hold K♣-K♠.

HellRaiser bets. There is $370 in the pot and it is $40 to you.

Question 7. Do you (a) fold (b) call (c) raise?

(a) ☐   (b) ☐   (c) ☐   Points: ....

You raise. Banjo folds, but Gazza thinks for a while and then calls. Hell-Raiser also calls.

River

The river is Q♣-9♥-8♣-4♦-9♦. You hold K♣-K♠.

HellRaiser checks. There is $570 in the pot and it is $40 to bet.

Question 8. Do you (a) check (b) bet?

(a) ☐   (b) ☐   Points: ....

          Total: ....

You bet. Both players call. Your kings stand up. Banjo squawks in the chat box that he folded a 9. The hand history shows that Gazza had Q♠-J♠ and HellRaiser had A♦-Q♥. Your excellent play has successfully protected your hand and won you a $690 pot.

♣ — ♥ — ♦ — ♠ — ♣ — ♥ — ♦ — ♠

SCORECHART

100	Outstanding. You found all the right moves to protect your hand.
90-99	Very good. You got the crucial things right.
80-89	Good. You handled your K-K well. Now all you need is to get dealt it more often.
70-79	You probably missed the plan to call the flop and raise the turn. This is an important tactic and you need to make sure you understand it.
60-69	You made a mess of this and may well have got outdrawn as a consequence. This is *very* expensive.
below 60	Poor.

♣ — ♥ — ♦ — ♠ — ♣ — ♥ — ♦ — ♠

ANSWERS AND ANALYSIS

Holding: K♣-K♠.

Question 1. (a) 10 (b) 8

In these tight games you will find it hard to draw players in if you open-raise UTG. Good players will just not give you any action. It is often a better play to limp, hoping for a raise, when you can three-bet and build a pot with your premium holding. Of course, you are running the risk that weaker hands will come in cheaply and may outdraw you. However, hands like K-K do not come along very often, and it is worth taking a risk to maximise your potential gains.

The two kings is a borderline holding for this play. With aces you can definitely limp if the game conditions justify it, whereas a pair of queens should always be opened with a raise as you are just too vulnerable with two possible overcards.

Question 2. (a) 3 (b) 10

In a tight game almost everyone is going to respect you UTG raise. However, raising from middle position is a different proposition. Players will expect you to open with a much wider range of hands and will be more inclined to give you action.

Question 3. (a) 2 (b) 10

These loose players are going to give you action whether you limp or raise. There is no point limping and running the risk of letting them in cheaply, when they are itching to play their suited connectors and small pairs anyway.

Flop: Q♣-9♥-8♣. You hold K♣-K♠.

Question 4. (a) 1 (b) 5

At least the dreaded ace has not appeared, but this is a rather ugly flop for you anyway. Three highest cards that form part of a straight, and a two-flush as well. It is quite possible that you are already behind and, even if not, there are going to be a considerable number of bad cards for you to avoid. This is not the time to risk giving free cards.

Question 5. (a) 0 (b) 20 (c) 14

You may well have the best hand, and there is something to be said for raising for value. However, there are a number of horrible cards that can hit on the turn, and it is better to await developments. If your raise were likely to blow Banjo and Gazza out of the pot, then it would be worth doing. However, if you re-raise, there will be $310 in the pot and it will be 'only' $40 for them to call. Even quite weak draws are getting the right price to call here.

Question 6. (a) 10 (b) 0 (c) 2

It is a rather a long shot that none of your opponents have a jack. Suited combinations of K-J, Q-J, J-T and J-9 are all typical hands that weak players will play, and HellRaiser could easily have played such a hand for one bet from the big blind. Books often advise that when the pot gets big you have to call down with any sort of hand, but this argument does not apply here. Even in the unlikely event of nobody holding a jack, your hand is still pretty worthless. Someone could easily have two pair or a set, and you have very few outs against such holdings.

If you are going to play you should raise in the hope that you can beat HellRaiser, and that Banjo and Gazza may fold if they hold two-pair hands. The argument for doing this would be stronger if Banjo and Gazza were tough players who could muck such hands, but they aren't and they won't.

Turn: Q♣-9♥-8♣-4♦. You hold K♣-K♠.

Question 7. (a) 0 (b) 10 (c) 25

This is the key moment of the hand, and this is the play that you prepared by calling (instead of re-raising) when HellRaiser bet the flop. The 4♦ is an excellent card for you, and this is the time to try and blow the opposition out of the pot. By waiting for the turn to raise you are confronting Banjo and Gazza with an $80 bet to stay in a pot of $450. They are getting odds of around 5½-to-1 to call. This means that they need around eight or nine outs to get value for a call, and even they may think twice about calling with hands such as A-9, A-8, Q-T, T-9 etc. There is a good chance you are beating HellRaiser, and if you can elbow Banjo and Gazza out of this large pot your equity in it will increase dramatically.

River: Q♣-9♥-8♣-4♦-9♦. You hold K♣-K♠.

Question 8. (a) 4 (b) 10

It is possible someone has a 9, and the pot is so big that you will have to call if you get raised. However, the upside of the pot being so big is that you will entice calls even from quite weak hands. You must bet here.

♣ — ♥ — ♦ — ♠ — ♣ — ♥ — ♦ — ♠

TIP: In this hand you could have three-bet the flop, which would have been good in terms of betting your hand for value. However, resisting this temptation created the opportunity to cripple the drawing hands on the turn. Watch out for this tactic. It can often result in winning a big pot that might otherwise have slipped through your fingers — and such swings are huge.

Hand 15

Getting Heat

♣ — ♥ — ♦ — ♠ — ♣ — ♥ — ♦ — ♠

INTRODUCTION

This is an eight-player $20-$40 game. You are two off the button with 9♣-9♠. The button is BabyJane, a soft, weak player, who is rather loose both before and after the flop. He is a shy player who spends much of his poker career in check-call mode. The big blind is Volcano, a maniac whom we met in Hand 3. Volcano likes to liven things up with random raises, and often tries to take down pots by barging everyone else out of them.

THE PLAY

Pre-flop

Hypothetical Pre-flop 1

Jackson – a sensible player – open-raises UTG. It is passed around to you. There is $70 in the pot and it is $40 to you.

Question 1. Do you (a) fold (b) call (c) raise?

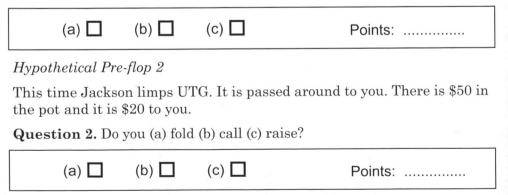

| (a) ☐ | (b) ☐ | (c) ☐ | Points: .... |

Hypothetical Pre-flop 2

This time Jackson limps UTG. It is passed around to you. There is $50 in the pot and it is $20 to you.

Question 2. Do you (a) fold (b) call (c) raise?

| (a) ☐ | (b) ☐ | (c) ☐ | Points: .... |

Hypothetical Pre-flop 3

This time Headstrong – a loose, aggressive player – open-raises one spot in front of you. There is $70 in the pot and it is $40 to you.

Question 3. Do you (a) fold (b) call (c) raise?

(a) ☐	(b) ☐	(c) ☐	Points: ....

Actual Pre-flop

It is passed around to you. There is $30 in the pot and it is $20 to you.

Question 4. Do you (a) fold (b) call (c) raise?

(a) ☐	(b) ☐	(c) ☐	Points: ....

You open-raise. BabyJane calls, the small blind folds and Volcano now – not entirely surprisingly – three-bets. All this tells you is that Volcano has a hand which is at least worth a call. You know from experience that he has reasonable pre-flop standards in terms of choosing the hands he wants to play – it is just that he invariably uses them to raise rather than just call. Of course, he may also have a premium hand, worthy of a three-bet. Only time will tell. There is $150 in the pot and it is $20 to you.

Question 5. Do you (a) fold (b) call (c) raise?

(a) ☐	(b) ☐	(c) ☐	Points: ....

You call, as does BabyJane.

Flop

The flop is J♣-J♥-3♠. You hold 9♣-9♠.

Shockingly, Volcano now bets. There is $210 in the pot and it is $20 to you.

Question 6. Do you (a) fold (b) call (c) raise?

(a) ☐	(b) ☐	(c) ☐	Points: ....

You raise. BabyJane thinks for a moment and then calls. Volcano doesn't think at all and re-raises. There is $330 in the pot and it is $20 to you.

Question 7. Do you (a) fold (b) call (c) cap the betting?

(a) ☐	(b) ☐	(c) ☐	Points: ....

You call, as does BabyJane. There is now $370 in the pot.

Turn

Hypothetical Turn

The turn is J♣-J♥-3♠-9♥. You hold 9♣-9♠.

Volcano bets. There is $410 in the pot and it is $40 to you.

Question 8. Do you (a) fold (b) call (c) raise?

(a) ☐	(b) ☐	(c) ☐	Points: ....

Actual Turn

The turn is J♣-J♥-3♠-4♥. You hold 9♣-9♠.

Volcano bets. There is $410 in the pot and it is $40 to you.

Question 9. Do you (a) fold (b) call (c) raise?

(a) ☐	(b) ☐	(c) ☐	Points: ....

You fold and BabyJane calls. Your involvement in the pot is over, but you watch with interest as the river brings J♣-J♥-3♠-4♥-8♦. Volcano bets. I am now going to reveal to you Volcano's hand. He has K♥-J♦.

Question 10. From your point of view, which hand would you like Baby-Jane to hold (a) Q♣-J♠ (b) A♣-J♠ (c) 8♠-8♥?

(a) ☐	(b) ☐	(c) ☐	Points: ....
			Total: ....

♣ — ♥ — ♦ — ♠ — ♣ — ♥ — ♦ — ♠

SCORECHART

100	Excellent. It is never easy to find the right plays against maniacs.
90-99	Very good. You played your hand hard and then dumped it at just the right moment.
80-89	Good.
70-79	You probably fell between two stools, not knowing whether to bet your hand for value or dump it.
60-69	These medium pairs are fiddly hands to play. There are nearly always overcards on the flop, and it is hard to know where you stand.
below 60	Poor.

♣ — ♥ — ♦ — ♠ — ♣ — ♥ — ♦ — ♠

ANSWERS AND ANALYSIS

Holding: 9♣-9♠.

Question 1. (a) 10 (b) 3 (c) 3

Your pair of 9s is just not quite good enough against a sensible early pre-flop raiser, especially with four players yet to act. Admittedly this is only an eight-handed table rather than a full ring game, but Jackson was first to speak, which would place him in early position even in a full ring game. It is best to fold.

Question 2. (a) 0 (b) 4 (c) 10

You probably have the best hand, and now you want put pressure on the blinds – and, indeed, the cut-off and button. Your hand has a decent chance of holding up unimproved against one or two opponents, but as more players enter the pot it becomes more likely that you will need to flop a set to win – and this is obviously a long-shot. Your raise offers a decent chance of that you can keep the number of opponents down to one or two.

Question 3. (a) 8 (b) 2 (c) 10

I don't like calling here, for the same reasons given in the answer to the previous question, but I think it is a very close decision between raising and folding. On balance I would probably raise, but it is hard to criticise a fold here, as you are unlikely to be much of a favourite in the pot. If Headstrong has random high cards it is likely they will both be bigger than 9, so in that case it is only 50/50 for your hand to hold up by the river. If he has a pair it is again probably about 50/50 whether they are bigger than your 9s. However, raising takes the initiative, and there is also the blind money to be played for. Since Headstrong is loose and aggressive, I slightly prefer raising to folding, but it is close.

Question 4. (a) 0 (b) 1 (c) 5

Your hand is good enough to open-raise UTG, so it is certainly good enough to raise here.

In fact, you must open-raise with your pocket 9s with only four players behind you. You probably have the best hand, but you are very vulnerable to overcards once the flop comes. By raising you may eliminate players and prevent the blinds from getting a free/cheap flop. If everyone folds that is fine. If you can eliminate some players and get it heads-up that is good also. But you don't want to just limp in and invite the cut-off, the button, and the blinds to come in cheaply and outdraw you. With pocket 9s you want to either take the flop short-handed with only one or maybe two opponents, or take it with a lot of opponents so that you are getting odds to try and flop a set. But the worst thing is to play pocket 9s with three or four opponents.

Question 5. (a) 0 (b) 5 (c) 3

If you could be sure that a raise would remove BabyJane from the fray, then it would be worthwhile. However, BabyJane initially called two bets cold and is unlikely to give up now just for another two bets. You can see the flop for just one further bet. and there seems little reason not to do so.

Flop: J♣-J♥-3♠. You hold 9♣-9♠.

Question 6. (a) 0 (b) 5 (c) 15

If no-one has a jack then you are probably winning, but your hand is vulnerable to overcards on the turn or river. If this is the case and you just call, BabyJane may well call along with just a couple of high cards. This is a big pot and you need to try and protect your holding. BabyJane will probably not want to call two bets cold with just overcards when there is a danger that he is drawing more or less dead if anyone holds a jack.

Question 7. (a) 1 (b) 10 (c) 0

This is beginning to look rather fishy. There are no drawing possibilities whatsoever with this flop, and yet BabyJane has called two bets cold on the flop and Volcano has erupted with yet another raise. Nevertheless, assuming that BabyJane will also call, there is $350 to be played for, and you can call for just $20. You almost have pot odds to try and snag a 9 on the turn. The implied odds are also rather good, because a 9 will not look like a threatening card, and you can be sure of picking up a few big bets if you get lucky and make the full house.

Question 8. (a) 0 (b) 0 (c) 5

One of the delights of online play is that it is now quite permissible to punch the air and shout 'Yes!' when you hit your hand. Having got this out of your system, you need to focus on the best way to get money into the pot, and this is almost certainly by raising. If BabyJane has a jack he will, at the very least, call and may even raise. Meanwhile, even if Baby-Jane just calls, Volcano may have A-J and re-raise. Raising could gain you a ton of bets. The most that calling can achieve is to lure BabyJane in for one extra bet if he doesn't have very much. Of course, BabyJane may have something like A-J and raise after you call. However, with a holding like that BabyJane is along for the ride anyway, so why not raise and bump the stakes up as much as possible.

When the pot is huge, it is nearly always utterly pointless to 'slowplay' hands. The opposition is getting enormous pot odds, and they will call along with the slightest chance of winning the pot.

Turn: J♣-J♥-3♠-4♥. You hold 9♣-9♠.

Question 9. (a) 20 (b) 4 (c) 0

Back to reality, where hitting two-outers is what other people do to you rather than you to them. You are losing this pot for sure. Volcano is a maniac, but even maniacs find a hand sometimes – and it looks like this might be his time. He can see the board just as well as you and has just three-bet out of position and then led out. Even if he has 'only' a big pair, he is still beating you. Meanwhile, there is also BabyJane to consider. It is hard to know what BabyJane has, but he did call two bets cold on the flop, which would be a typical play for a weak player who has made trips and plans to raise on the turn when the bet size doubles. A more tricky player might have three-bet on the flop to disguise their hand.

Having decided that you are losing, you can see that you are playing a two-outer. A two-outer is about a 22-to-1 against shot. You have to put in $40, and would thus need around $880 in the pot to make this call worthwhile. There is nowhere near that amount in there. If you do happen to hit, the implied odds are rather good, but even so, this does not merit a call. One further problem is that BabyJane may raise if you call, and that would be simply awful. Fold.

Question 10. (a) 0 (b) 3 (c) 10

You are out of the pot and you know that you made a good fold so, in principle, you do not really care who wins. However, assuming that you are not about to quit the game, you will be playing more pots against these players. It does not really matter much to you if BabyJane wins the pot or not – he will continue to play his soft weak game and will continue to be a good target.

Volcano, however, is a different matter. Winning a good pot (a) will give him confidence and – as he is already aggressive – this will make him harder to play. If he loses having raised with a dominated hand (b) he will probably realise that he has only himself to blame. He may then be annoyed, and this could affect his play, but it is also possible that he will tighten up. However, if he suffers an appalling outdraw (c), he will be furious and – with a bit of luck – may go on tilt. That would be very good news indeed.

♣ — ♥ — ♦ — ♠ — ♣ — ♥ — ♦ — ♠

 TIP: You will always lose money to the maniacs. Always. The trick is to win it all back with interest. The best way to play a maniac is to recognise this fact. Play back at them hard but develop a feel for when they really do have a hand. Don't be afraid to muck your hand when it is obvious you are beaten.

Hand 16

Short Stacked

♣ — ♥ — ♦ — ♠ — ♣ — ♥ — ♦ — ♠

INTRODUCTION

This is a short-handed six-player $20-$40 game. You are in the cut-off with 8♣-7♣. This is a good game with soft players who are too loose pre-flop and tend to go to the river with pretty mediocre holdings. Billyboy, who is on the button, fits this description, although he is more aggressive then the other players at the table. Dave is on the big blind and has become short stacked. He now has only $60 left. In fact, having posted his blind, he is now down to precisely $40.

THE PLAY

Pre-flop

Hypothetical Pre-flop

Let's assume that the game is still six-handed, but now it is not such a good game and is populated by tight players. It is passed around to you. There is $30 in the pot and it is $20 to you.

Question 1. Do you (a) fold (b) call (c) raise?

(a) ☐	(b) ☐	(c) ☐	Points: ....

Actual Pre-flop

The game is now as described in the introduction. Again it is passed around to you. There is $30 in the pot and it is $20 to you.

Question 2. Do you (a) fold (b) call (c) raise?

(a) ☐	(b) ☐	(c) ☐	Points: ....

You raise, Billyboy calls and the small blind folds. Dave also calls from the big blind and now has just $20 remaining.

Flop

Hypothetical Flop

The flop is K♦-9♥-6♥. You hold 8♣-7♣.

Dave now bets out and is all-in. There is $150 in the pot and it is $20 to bet.

Question 3. Do you (a) fold (b) call (c) raise?

(a) ☐	(b) ☐	(c) ☐	Points: ....

Actual Flop

The flop is K♦-9♥-6♥. You hold 8♣-7♣.

Dave now checks. There is $130 in the pot and it is $20 to you.

Question 4. Do you (a) check (b) bet?

(a) ☐	(b) ☐	Points: ....

You bet. Billyboy calls, as does Dave who is now all-in.

Turn

Hypothetical Turn

The turn is K♦-9♥-6♥-A♠. You hold 8♣-7♣.

Let's assume that Dave has not allowed himself to become short-stacked and has plenty of money on the table. Dave now checks. There is $190 in the pot and it is $40 to you.

Question 5. Do you (a) check (b) bet?

(a) ☐	(b) ☐	Points: ....

Actual Turn

The turn is still K♦-9♥-6♥-A♠. You hold 8♣-7♣.

However, now Dave is cleaned out and has no money. He therefore cannot bet so the action passes to you. There is $190 in the pot and it is $40 to bet.

Question 6. Do you (a) check (b) bet?

(a) ☐   (b) ☐   Points: ....

You check. Billyboy now bets, placing $40 in a side pot. Dave, of course, cannot contribute. There is $190 in the main pot and $40 in the side pot, and it is $40 to you.

Question 7. Do you (a) fold (b) call (c) raise?

(a) ☐   (b) ☐   (c) ☐   Points: ....

You call.

River

The river is K♦-9♥-6♥-A♠-8♠. You hold 8♣-7♣.

There is $190 in the main pot and $80 in the side pot, and it is $40 to bet.

Question 8. Do you (a) check (b) bet?

(a) ☐   (b) ☐   Points: ....

You check and Billyboy now bets. There is $190 in the main pot and $120 in the side pot and it is $40 to you.

Question 9. Do you (a) fold (b) call (c) raise?

(a) ☐   (b) ☐   (c) ☐   Points: ....

                                   Total: ....

You fold. Billyboy shows A♦-9♦ for two pair, which beats Dave's K♠-Q♥.

SCORECHART

100	Excellent. Good handling of your weak draw.
90-99	Very good.
80-89	Good. You were aware of the problems of coping with the short stack.
70-79	You probably blundered on Question 6. Be very aware of short-stacked players.
60-69	You must have misunderstood the hand. Play through it again.
below 60	Poor.

♣ – ♥ – ♦ – ♠ – ♣ – ♥ – ♦ – ♠

ANSWERS AND ANALYSIS

Holding: 8♣-7♣.

Question 1. (a) 10 (b) 2 (c) 6

You have modest-sized suited connectors. These hands are generally only playable if you can get in cheaply, and have plenty of opponents. Generally you should fold these kinds of hands here. However, you are in the cut-off and – in a tight game – have a reasonable chance to steal the blinds if you open-raise. You may also just get a call from the big blind and then take the pot right away if he misses the flop. Despite all that, I feel this hand is just too weak – even with the blind-stealing opportunity – and it is best to ditch it.

Question 2. (a) 10 (b) 2 (c) 4

All the same arguments apply except that now – as your opponents are loose – you have even less of a chance to steal the blinds. In a game such as this you just want to play your big cards, make big pairs and get paid off by the draws and little pairs. There is no excuse for messing around in short-handed pots with feeble drawing hands.

Question 3. (a) 0 (b) 2 (c) 10

There are numerous drawing possibilities on this flop, and Dave is all-in and could have almost anything. You have flopped a straight draw and probably have eight outs (a third heart could make someone a flush). However, there are many possible holdings for Dave against which you have extra outs by making a pair, e.g. 6-x, a flush draw, a gutshot draw, or two random high cards not including a king. There is a very decent chance that your raise will force Billyboy out of the pot, which would be an excellent result. You then get $20 of your $40 back and achieve a free showdown against Dave with very decent chances, whatever he holds. Even if Billyboy calls or raises, you have a good draw with two cards to come.

Calling, in comparison, is rather feeble. Billyboy then has sufficient pot odds to justify calling with as few as six outs, and there are all sorts of holdings he can then call with that you would be bad news for you.

Flop: K♦-9♥-6♥. You hold 8♣-7♣.

Question 4. (a) 2 (b) 10

You are the pre-flop raiser, and the flop is quite a decent one for you. Bet now. You never know – they might both fold.

Question 5. (a) 4 (b) 10

These situations are tough. You have no made hand whatsoever, 'only' a draw, and you have to decide whether to keep firing at the pot. With one opponent I would say definitely go ahead and bet. With three opponents I would be very much inclined to check. Two, as here, is borderline. However, neither of your opponents has shown any strength at all in this pot, and the A♠ is a good scare card. Betting now may get someone to fold a 9 or even a king. Furthermore, if you get one opponent to fold and the other is on a draw then, assuming they miss their draw, a bet from you on the river has an excellent chance to take the pot.

Turn: K♦-9♥-6♥-A♠. You hold 8♣-7♣.

Question 6. (a) 25 (b) 5

This is a strange situation. When you have taken the initiative in a pot, suddenly switching into check-call mode is usually awful play. Here, however, it is completely justified and, in fact, a bet would be poor play. The crucial factor is that Dave is all-in and will get a free showdown for the main pot whatever happens. Thus, if your hand does not improve – and most likely you have just eight outs – you have absolutely no chance to win on the river.

There are, generally, two possible reasons to bet in a given situation:

a) You have the best hand, or a profitable draw, and want to get more money in the pot;

b) You want to force players out of the pot to improve your chances of winning. The best version of this is when you force all of your opponents out of the pot and win it at once.

Neither of these applies here:

a) Your 8-high is certainly not the best hand, nor is your open-ended straight a profitable draw;

b) Forcing Billyboy out of the pot does not improve your chances in the slightest, whereas it is impossible to force Dave out of the pot, since he is all-in.

Thus there is no reason to bet. If you check and Billyboy also checks, you have gained a free look at the river with your eight-outer, which would be an excellent result. Even if Billyboy bets, you can call for the pot odds. Note that your implied odds are quite good. If a 10 or 5 comes it will not look like a danger card, and you could easily pick up a further big bet or two from Billyboy on the river.

Note also that betting and getting raised by Billyboy would be most un-pleasant – you would still have a call for the pot odds, but you would have had to spend an additional $40.

Question 7. (a) 0 (b) 10 (c) 0

As planned. You have pot odds to draw to the straight. If you chose this moment (with Dave all-in) to make a semi-bluff check-raise with your 8-high then I would strongly recommend that you keep the day job.

River: K♦-9♥-6♥-A♠-8♠. You hold 8♣-7♣.

Question 8. (a) 5 (b) 0

Billyboy is not going to call with a worse hand than yours.

Question 9. (a) 10 (b) 1 (c) 0

If you were playing for the whole $310 pot then a crying call might just about be justified. However, even if by some miracle you are beating Billyboy, it is rather unlikely that your feeble pair will stand up against Dave's hand.

♣ — ♥ — ♦ — ♠ — ♣ — ♥ — ♦ — ♠

 TIP: Be very aware when a player becomes short-stacked. The fact that they can no longer bet – or be obliged to call bets – fundamentally changes the dynamics of the hand.

Hand 17

Top Pair, Top Kicker

♣ – ♥ – ♦ – ♠ – ♣ – ♥ – ♦ – ♠

INTRODUCTION

This is a ten-player $20-$40 game. You are in the small blind with
A♣-9♣. The cut-off is BladeRunner. BladeRunner is one of those untutored natural players. He is loose pre-flop and seems to have very little
idea of pre-flop strategy and hand values. However, he plays rather well
post-flop. The big blind is Pacman – a soft, weak player, who makes the
typical soft, weak errors – playing inferior cards and then calling along
when he gets a modest piece of the flop.

THE PLAY

Pre-flop

Hypothetical Pre-flop 1

Let's assume that BladeRunner is actually UTG and opens with a raise.
It is passed around to you. There is $70 in the pot and it is $30 to you.

Question 1. Do you (a) fold (b) call (c) raise?

(a) ☐	(b) ☐	(c) ☐	Points: ....

Hypothetical Pre-flop 2

It is passed around to BladeRunner, who is now firmly back in the cut-off
position. He opens with a raise. The button folds. There is $70 in the pot
and it is $30 to you.

Question 2. Do you (a) fold (b) call (c) raise?

| (a) ☐ | (b) ☐ | (c) ☐ | Points: .... |

Actual Pre-flop

It is passed around to BladeRunner, who limps. The button folds. There is $50 in the pot and it is $10 to you.

Question 3. Do you (a) fold (b) call (c) raise?

| (a) ☐ | (b) ☐ | (c) ☐ | Points: .... |

You raise. Pacman calls for $20, as does BladeRunner.

Flop

The flop is 9♥-7♦-5♣. You hold A♣-9♣.

You have top pair, top kicker, so you are unlikely to be folding just yet. There is $120 in the pot and it is $20 to bet. What is your preferred plan?

Question 4. Do you (a) check, planning to call (b) check, planning a check-raise (c) bet?

| (a) ☐ | (b) ☐ | (c) ☐ | Points: .... |

You bet, Pacman calls and BladeRunner now raises. There is $200 in the pot and it is $20 to you.

Question 5. Do you (a) fold (b) call (c) raise?

| (a) ☐ | (b) ☐ | (c) ☐ | Points: .... |

You raise. Pacman thinks for a moment but calls the two bets. BladeRunner now caps the betting. There is $320 in the pot and it is $20 to bet.

Question 6. Do you (a) fold (b) call?

| (a) ☐ | (b) ☐ | Points: .... |

You call, and so does Pacman.

Turn

Hypothetical Turn

The turn is 9♥-7♦-5♣-A♠. You hold A♣-9♣.

There is $360 in the pot and it is $40 to bet.

Question 7. Do you (a) check, planning to call (b) check, planning a check-raise (c) bet?

(a) ☐	(b) ☐	(c) ☐	Points: ....

Actual Turn

The turn is 9♥-7♦-5♣-2♥. You hold A♣-9♣.

There is $360 in the pot and it is $40 to bet.

Question 8. Do you (a) check (b) bet?

(a) ☐	(b) ☐	Points: ....

You check. Pacman also keeps quiet, but BladeRunner now bets. There is $400 in the pot and it is $40 to you.

Question 9. Do you (a) fold (b) call (c) raise?

(a) ☐	(b) ☐	(c) ☐	Points: ....
			Total: ....

You fold, but Pacman calls. The river brings 9♥-7♦-5♣-2♥-K♠. Pacman checks and calls BladeRunner's bet. BladeRunner shows down 9♠-7♠, which takes the pot. The hand history shows that Pacman had 8♦-7♣.

♣ — ♥ — ♦ — ♠ — ♣ — ♥ — ♦ — ♠

SCORECHART

100   Excellent. You know when to pump and when to dump.

90-99   Very good. You didn't miss much.

80-89   Good. You got the important things right.

70-79   Average. Don't fall in love with top pair, top kicker.

60-69   You either released the hand too early or too late.

below 60   Poor.

♣ – ♥ – ♦ – ♠ – ♣ – ♥ – ♦ – ♠

ANSWERS AND ANALYSIS

Holding: A♣-9♣.

Question 1. (a) 10 (b) 2 (c) 4

Against a normal opponent this hand is definitely a fold, as there is just too great a danger that your hand is dominated. If he is open-raising with A-x, then 'x' is almost certainly better than your 9, and you will have to hit your 9 and dodge overcards. If he has a pair it is likely to be higher than your 9, so you will have to hit an ace. Even then you will still find it difficult to take the initiative, as you will fear be afraid that a bigger ace is out against you. Of course, you might make a flush or two pair, but these possibilities are just too remote to overcome the unfavourable pot odds.

Although we know that BladeRunner has strange pre-flop values, this hand is still a fold. Even players with poor pre-flop values tend to be cautious when UTG in a full ring game. Of course, a raise might work but, unless you have a really good line on BladeRunner, it just feels too risky. Furthermore, Pacman has yet to speak and you will also have bad position for the whole hand. Dump it.

Question 2. (a) 6 (b) 2 (c) 10

BladeRunner is now in the cut-off, which is entirely different proposition from facing a raise from him UTG. On the balance of probabilities your hand is likely better than his, and you should raise to put pressure on Pacman. If you just call, Pacman will call with almost anything, and you will probably have to make a real hand to win. If you can get Pacman out, your chances to take the pot increase substantially. Your three-bet, out of position, is a strong move, and you will bet the flop no matter what comes. If BladeRunner hasn't connected, he may well fold at once.

Having said all that, I don't think that folding is a terrible play either, as your hand is not really much to write home about.

Question 3. (a) 0 (b) 4 (c) 10

Well, you could see the flop cheaply with a call (Pacman is unlikely to raise), but BladeRunner's limp suggests a rather weedy hand, and you are probably winning. It is best to raise. You may even get Pacman out or, at least, oblige him to pay an extra $20 to see the flop with a feeble holding.

Flop: 9♥-7♦-5♣. You hold A♣-9♣.

Question 4. (a) 0 (b) 4 (c) 10

The flop is undoubtedly a good one for you, but the coordinated nature of the three cards is dangerous. You are vulnerable to almost anything coming on the turn: an overcard (not an ace) could make a higher pair, and any card between a 9 and 5 could make someone a straight, trips or even two pair. This is not the time to give a free card, so it is best to bet out.

Checking could work for you if Pacman also checks and BladeRunner then bets. You could then raise and force Pacman to call two bets to continue. However, BladeRunner only limped originally and may well decide to take a free card.

Note also that you raised pre-flop, out of position, and this announces a good holding. It is natural to follow this up with a flop bet, almost regardless of what comes. If you now check it will look a little suspicious, and will perhaps encourage your opponents to take the free card. You have a decent hand, but the best result would be to take down the pot at once. Bet.

Question 5. (a) 0 (b) 5 (c) 15

BladeRunner's raise is not particularly worrying. He could easily have a 9 with a worse kicker or a drawing hand such as 8-7 or 7-6. Pacman could easily have called on the flop with almost anything, but now you will force him to pay two bets to continue. Either he will fold, which will improve your pot equity, or he will call with inadequate values.

Question 6. (a) 0 (b) 5

It is remarkable how quickly the assessment of your chances can change. The flop was looking rather good for you, but now the whole hand has turned into an ugly mess and you haven't even seen the turn card yet. You three-bet out of position, but BladeRunner isn't impressed. It is likely that your hand is behind, and even if you improve you will still have to be cautious. Nevertheless, it would be very odd play to fold here with 16-to-1 pot odds. Note that you have a backdoor flush possibility, which is a small but significant contribution to your chances.

Question 7. (a) 5 (b) 0 (c) 15

It may turn out to be rather uncomfortable for you, but you must bet here, as there is a decent chance that you have just outdrawn BladeRunner. If he holds 9-7, 9-5 or 7-5 this has indeed happened. Alternatively, if he holds 7-7, 5-5 or 8-6 then you will face a raise, which you will call with your four-outer.

You must bet here as the pot has suddenly become rather large, and you do not want to run the risk of giving Pacman – who is probably holding some feeble drawing hand – a free card.

Turn: 9♥-7♦-5♣-2♥. You hold A♣-9♣.

Question 8. (a) 5 (b) 0

Betting here is the poker equivalent of the Charge of the Light Brigade. Please have some respect for the opposition's betting.

Question 9. (a) 20 (b) 5 (c) 0

There is now $400 in the pot and it costs you $40 to call. This is pot odds of 10-to-1. On a good day, you may have five outs with any ace or 9, which would justify a call. However, the trouble is that these outs may not win for you. It is possible that you are up against a made straight, in which case you are drawing dead. Although unlikely, you could also be up against a set, in which case you are also drawing dead. Furthermore, if BladeRunner has 9-7 (or maybe 9-5, although that would be a strange hand to limp with), your only out is an ace, and the odds are not there to chase it. One final consideration is that Pacman, who has spent the entire time limping along, is still in the pot, and you cannot be sure what he has. It is time to abandon ship.

♣ – ♥ – ♦ – ♠ – ♣ – ♥ – ♦ – ♠

 TIP: As you may have observed, hold'em can be a very frustrating game. You flop top pair, top kicker and it turns out that some weak player has outdrawn you, and you are stuck with a bad trap hand. In such situations, many players unthinkingly pay off to the river. Do not fall into this trap. Judge each hand on its merits. Top pair, top kicker is often an excellent hand, but there is no law that says you have to take it to the river whatever comes.

Hand 18

Bright Button

♣ — ♥ — ♦ — ♠ — ♣ — ♥ — ♦ — ♠

INTRODUCTION

This is a ten-player $15-$30 game. You are on the button with K♦-J♦. You are not terribly familiar with the opposition, but this seems to be an archetypal good game. Most of the players are fairly loose and are going too far with second-rate hands. NYBoy, AcesUp and KingKong are all in middle position, and are each typical players for this game.

THE PLAY

Pre-flop

Hypothetical Pre-flop 1

It is passed around to NYBoy, who limps in. AcesUp and KingKong also limp, and it is folded to you on the button. Let's change your hand to Q♦-10♦. There is $70 in the pot and it is $15 to you.

Question 1. Do you (a) fold (b) call (c) raise?

(a) ☐	(b) ☐	(c) ☐	Points: ....

Hypothetical Pre-flop 2

The action is the same as before, but now your hand is 5♦-5♣. There is $70 in the pot and it is $15 to you.

Question 2. Do you (a) fold (b) call (c) raise?

(a) ☐	(b) ☐	(c) ☐	Points: ....

Actual Pre-flop

The action is the same as before, and now you have your proper hand – K♦-J♦. There is $70 in the pot and it is $15 to you.

Question 3. Do you (a) fold (b) call (c) raise?

(a) ☐   (b) ☐   (c) ☐   Points: ....

You raise. The blinds both fold, and all three limpers call. There is now $145 in the pot.

Flop

Hypothetical Flop

The flop is Q♥-9♣-5♦. You hold K♦-J♦.

NYBoy checks, but AcesUp bets and KingKong raises. There is $190 in the pot and it is $30 to you.

Question 4. Do you (a) fold (b) call (c) raise?

(a) ☐   (b) ☐   (c) ☐   Points: ....

Actual Flop

The flop is again Q♥-9♣-5♦. You hold K♦-J♦.

NYBoy checks, but AcesUp bets and KingKong just calls. There is $175 in the pot and it is $15 to you.

Question 5. Do you (a) fold (b) call (c) raise?

(a) ☐   (b) ☐   (c) ☐   Points: ....

You raise. NYBoy folds, and AcesUp and KingKong both call.

Turn

Hypothetical Turn

The turn is Q♥-9♣-5♦-2♦. You hold K♦-J♦.

It is checked to you. There is $235 in the pot and it is $30 to bet.

Question 6. Do you (a) check (b) bet?

(a) ☐   (b) ☐   Points: ....

Actual Turn

The turn is Q♥-9♣-5♦-6♠. You hold K♦-J♦.

AcesUp and KingKong both check. There is $235 in the pot and it is $30 to bet.

Question 7. Do you (a) check (b) bet?

(a) ☐	(b) ☐	Points: ....

You check.

River

The river is Q♥-9♣-5♦-6♠-10♠. You hold K♦-J♦.

AcesUp and KingKong both check. There is $235 in the pot and it is $30 to bet.

Question 8. Do you (a) check (b) bet?

(a) ☐	(b) ☐	Points: ....
		Total: ....

You bet. Much to your delight both players call and, of course, you take the pot. AcesUp had K♠-9♠, and KingKong had a feeble 7♥-7♠.

♣ — ♥ — ♦ — ♠ — ♣ — ♥ — ♦ — ♠

SCORECHART

100	Excellent. You appreciated the value of your good position.
90-99	Very good.
80-89	Good. This is a solid score and demonstrated that you valued your holding and position accurately.
70-79	You were probably too passive. With position and a draw always be aware of the possibility of trying for a free card.
60-69	You were almost certainly too passive.
below 60	Poor.

♣ — ♥ — ♦ — ♠ — ♣ — ♥ — ♦ — ♠

ANSWERS AND ANALYSIS

Holding: K♦-J♦.

Question 1. (a) 0 (b) 10 (c) 6

You have good position and a moderate hand. You can call happily enough, but raising is too frisky. You have straight and flush possibilities, but your holding is dominated by hands as weak as Q-J and K-10, which are quite likely holdings for middle position limpers.

Question 2. (a) 2 (b) 10 (c) 4

With three players already in, you will very likely need to flop a set to win. If you call and both blinds play you are getting pot odds of 5-to-1, but the chances of flopping a set are approximately 7½-to-1. However, your implied odds are excellent, and you could rake in a decent pot if you do hit. Calling is thus fine and folding is rather feeble.

Some players might like to raise here on the grounds that with a larger pot they are more likely to get good action if they hit a set. Also if the flop is of no help, there is a possibility that they might be able to take a free card for the (small) extra chance of hitting the set on the turn. However, by raising, you are putting an extra $15 into the pot in an attempt to win an extra $45 or maybe $60 if one blind calls. The extra bet does not pay you the odds you need to flop a set, and the small advantages that accrue from raising do not really outweigh this. With five limpers in you could certainly consider raising, but three is too few.

Question 3. (a) 0 (b) 5 (c) 15

This is a good hand with which to raise. It plays well in a multi-way pot and is much less likely to be dominated than Q♦-10♦ (as in Question 1). Your K-J holding is only dominated by A-K, A-J or K-Q, and anyone with a hand this strong may well have raised before you. Playing K-J suited on the button in an unraised pot definitely has a positive expectation. The limpers in front of you could have very mediocre holdings, and you should make them pay extra to see the flop.

Question 4. (a) 15 (b) 5 (c) 2

It is rather a shame to fold, but $30 is too much to pay here. You need approximately seven or eight outs to justify calling for the pot odds, and your only clean out is to a 10. With a bet and a raise before you it is highly likely that someone has a queen, so hitting a jack is probably useless. You might have an out to a king, but even this is not certain, as the following holdings will scupper you: K-Q, J-10 and K-9. Even if neither opponent has one of these combinations, a king will still create redraws on the river. You should not count you king as more than about 1½ outs, and even this may be a little generous. You thus have about 5½ outs and, even if you add on a little for the backdoor flush draw, it is hard to justify a call. There is also the slight worry that NYBoy or AcesUp may re-raise.

Raising might be okay if you could be sure it would buy you a free card, but this is far from certain. Also, as previously discussed, you may not have all that many outs. It is best to let it go.

Flop: Q♥-9♣-5♦. You hold K♦-J♦.

Question 5. (a) 0 (b) 4 (c) 15

The fact that KingKong just called instead of raising makes all the difference, and now it is justified for you to take the initiative in the pot. You are probably playing at least seven outs, and the generally passive play of your opponents to date should encourage you to keep the momentum going. AcesUp probably has something reasonable, although this may be as little as a 9, whereas KingKong could have just about anything, but is unlikely to be interfering with your draws. This is a good moment to raise and create the possibility of taking a free card on the turn.

Question 6. (a) 5 (b) 15

The 2♦ is a good card for you, creating numerous extra outs with the flush draw. It is also most unlikely to have helped an opponent. You now have so many outs, probably at least 15, that maintaining the initiative with a bet is justified.

Turn: Q♥-9♣-5♦-6♠. You hold K♦-J♦.

Question 7. (a) 15 (b) 5

The 6♠ does nothing for your hand, and may have helped an opponent. If one of them was playing a gutshot draw between the 9 and 5 they have now made at least a pair. Also the hands J-8 and 10-8 have now picked up four extra outs with the gutshot. You certainly do not have the best hand here, and a bet is unlikely to force your opponents out, whilst also risking a nasty check-raise. It is best to take the free card.

River: Q♥-9♣-5♦-6♠-10♠. You hold K♦-J♦.

Question 8. (a) 0 (b) 5

Hold'em is not always a struggle to try and decide how to play a mediocre hand – sometimes you hit the nuts. Not very often, but it happens. The only slight disappointment is that both your opponents checked the river, despite the fact that you showed weakness on the turn.

♣ — ♥ — ♦ — ♠ — ♣ — ♥ — ♦ — ♠

TIP: Holding position on your opponents creates all sorts of opportunities. Hands that would be rather vulnerable in early position become much stronger from the cut-off or button. Be aware of opportunities to bet and raise to apply pressure or perhaps take a free card.

Hand 19

Drawing Conclusions

♣ — ♥ — ♦ — ♠ — ♣ — ♥ — ♦ — ♠

INTRODUCTION

This is an eight-player $15-$30 game. You are on the small blind with
Q♦-J♣. This is a solid game. The opposition does not appear to be bril-
liant, but they all seem to be playing decent cards. No-one has made any
surprising moves, and they all seem to bet their hands for value. Typical
of these players are TheDevil, who is UTG, and RisingSun, who is in the
big blind.

THE PLAY

Pre-flop

TheDevil limps in for $15, and it is passed around to you. There is $40 in
the pot and it is $5 to you.

Question 1. Do you (a) fold (b) call (c) raise?

(a) ☐	(b) ☐	(c) ☐	Points: ....

You call and RisingSun raises. TheDevil calls. There is $75 in the pot and
it is $15 to you.

Question 2. Do you (a) fold (b) call (c) raise?

(a) ☐	(b) ☐	(c) ☐	Points: ....

You call.

Flop

The flop is 10♦-9♣-3♣. You hold Q♦-J♣.

There is $90 in the pot and it is $15 to bet.

Question 3. Do you (a) check, planning a call (b) check, planning a check-raise (c) bet?

(a) ☐   (b) ☐   (c) ☐   Points: ....

You bet and both of your opponents call.

Turn

Hypothetical Turn

Let's assume that the preceding action has been slightly different. Pre-flop, RisingSun checked from the big blind (rather than raising). The flop action was then identical, with you betting out and both other players calling.

The turn is 10♦-9♣-3♣-7♦. You hold Q♦-J♣.

There is $90 in the pot and it is $30 to bet.

Question 4. Do you (a) check (b) bet?

(a) ☐   (b) ☐   Points: ....

You check.

Hypothetical Turn continued

RisingSun thinks for a while and bets. TheDevil now raises. There is $180 in the pot and it is $60 to you.

Question 5. Do you (a) fold (b) call (c) raise?

(a) ☐   (b) ☐   (c) ☐   Points: ....

Actual Turn

The action is now back as it was with RisingSun's pre-flop raise, which both you and TheDevil called. The turn is again 10♦-9♣-3♣-7♦. You hold Q♦-J♣.

There is $135 in the pot and it is $30 to bet.

Question 6. Do you (a) check (b) bet?

(a) ☐   (b) ☐   Points: ....

You bet.

The action now continues in similar vein to the hypothetical turn. RisingSun thinks for a moment and raises. TheDevil now re-raises. There is $315 in the pot and it is $60 to you.

Question 7. Do you (a) fold (b) call (c) raise?

(a) ☐   (b) ☐   (c) ☐   Points: ....

You call. RisingSun caps the betting and TheDevil calls. There is $465 in the pot and it is $30 to you.

Question 8. Do you (a) fold (b) call?

(a) ☐   (b) ☐   Points: ....

You call.

River

Hypothetical River

The river is 10♦-9♣-3♣-7♦-K♣. You hold Q♦-J♣.

There is $495 in the pot and it is $30 to bet.

Question 9. Do you (a) check (b) bet?

(a) ☐   (b) ☐   Points: ....

Actual River

The river is 10♦-9♣-3♣-7♦-K♠. You hold Q♦-J♣.

There is $495 in the pot and it is $30 to bet.

Question 10. Do you (a) check (b) bet?

(a) ☐   (b) ☐   Points: ....

You check. RisingSun bets and The Devil thinks for a moment and calls. There is $555 in the pot and it is $30 to you.

Question 11. Do you (a) fold (b) call (c) raise?

(a) ☐	(b) ☐	(c) ☐	Points: ....
			Total: ....

You raise. RisingSun calls and TheDevil agonises until his time nearly runs out and folds. Obviously, you hold the nuts and take the pot. RisingSun had 9♠-9♥ and flopped a set.

♣ — ♥ — ♦ — ♠ — ♣ — ♥ — ♦ — ♠

SCORECHART

100   Outstanding. There were many tough decisions here.

90-99   Excellent. Very good handling of a difficult drawing hand.

80-89   Very respectable. You must have got the important things right.

70-79   You may have been too crude in your assessment of your outs.

60-69   Never mind. If you hung around long enough you hit the nuts and got the money.

below 60 Poor.

♣ — ♥ — ♦ — ♠ — ♣ — ♥ — ♦ — ♠

ANSWERS AND ANALYSIS

Holding: Q♦-J♣.

Question 1. (a) 0 (b) 5 (c) 1

You have a moderate hand and an easy call. Some players might like to raise to put pressure on the big blind, but this seems a little over the top. It is quite likely you will get 8-to-1 pot odds with your cheap call. It is hard to believe that raising offers better value.

Question 2. (a) 0 (b) 5 (c) 0

The raise is unfortunate, but it is still an easy call for you.

Flop: 10♦-9♣-3♣. You hold Q♦-J♣.

Question 3. (a) 4 (b) 2 (c) 15

You have hit a very decent flop with an open-ended straight draw and two overcards. You cannot be sure how many outs you have, but it is a minimum of six (there is a potential flush draw) and – on a good day –

could be as many as 14. It is quite possible that RisingSun raised with big cards, and if so this flop probably missed him. Thus it is best to put pressure on him with a bet. The flop is mildly coordinated, and if he has A-K or A-Q he may not like the look of it and you could get him out. This would be very good news, whatever TheDevil decides to do.

It would be very feeble to check-call here. You have easily enough of a hand to call and, with all those possible outs, you don't fear a raise, so why not bet? You never know – they might both fold.

Checking with the intention of check-raising seems way too much. This would build the pot, which will be more likely to tie the players to their hands. You will then be forced to hit your hand to win. You have a decent draw but nothing more, so there is little to be gained by building the pot.

The mathematics of the situation bears this out. You don't know how many outs you have, but nine would be a reasonable assumption. This would occur if the flush draw were live, but you also had one overcard out. With nine outs your chances of making your hand by the river is approximately 33%. Thus, with two callers you have fair value for any bet, but no more. Thus, if you check-raise and tie players to the pot, you will 'only' be getting value for your hand. If you bet you keep the size of the pot down, and slightly improve your chances of winning without making your hand. This gives you an equity edge and explains why leading out is a better play.

Question 4. (a) 15 (b) 6

Unfortunately, your flop bet didn't get anyone out, and the turn card has not been favourable. It does nothing for your hand, but there is some chance it has assisted the opposition. If there were a chance of taking the pot down with a bet, I would certainly recommend continuing to fire. However, the play so far suggests that this is unlikely. Both players have quietly called your flop bet, and this suggests that one of them is possibly lurking in the weeds, waiting to hit you with a turn raise. If you check and there is a bet and a call, you have an easy call. However, if you lead out and get raised you will end up paying over the odds for your draw.

It is peculiar to take the initiative in a pot and then meekly surrender it to go into check-call mode. However, this play is the best way to guarantee value for your draw.

Question 5. (a) 10 (b) 4 (c) 0

Your check was good play, and this has enabled you to get away from the hand cheaply. Facing a $60 bet the pot is offering you 3-to-1, so you need around 12-13 outs to get value. You now have only four cards that will deliver the absolute nuts, since another potential flush draw has appeared. Meanwhile, TheDevil has announced a big hand and this seriously taints your outs.

For example, if RisingSun has a flush draw and TheDevil has a two pair hand or better (and this is likely), then you are restricted to six outs. Even if there is no flush draw out against you and you have eight outs, this still does not represent good value. Admittedly, your opponents cannot have everything, but you have to appreciate that your holding is now seriously devalued.

A further small point is that if an 8 comes to make your straight, it will put four cards to a straight on the board which will weaken your implied odds, since no-one is going to bet without a jack in their hand.

There is also the further problem that RisingSun may re-raise, which would be awful for you. You have a good-looking draw, and it is a pity to dump it, but the odds are just not there to play.

Turn: 10♦-9♣-3♣-7♦. You hold Q♦-J♣.

Question 6. (a) 8 (b) 10

This is a very close call, since there is now a bit more money in the pot than in the previous example, which just about justifies taking a pop at it. Also RisingSun raised pre-flop and then just called on the flop. This suggests that he may well hold A-K or A-Q and didn't connect with the flop and, if so, the turn has also not helped. When he checked pre-flop and just called on the flop he could hold almost anything, and the 7♦ is then much more likely to be helpful for him.

Question 7. (a) 4 (b) 10 (c) 0

The pot odds are now much better and calling is not really a difficult decision. You can assume that RisingSun will call, so you are betting $60 into a pot of $345. You thus need around six or seven outs, and you certainly have value here.

Question 8. (a) 0 (b) 5

Not much to think about there.

Question 9. (a) 4 (b) 10

The way you have played the hand strongly suggests that you may be on a flush draw. If your opponents are alert, they are likely to check even if they have quite big (but non-flush) hands. It is, of course, possible that one of them has now made a flush and you are losing, but that does not seem likely on the play. Both players showed the kind of aggression on the turn that indicates a decent made hand rather than a drawing one. Bet now – the pot is big and you will pick up crying calls. If you check it may get checked around, and these bets well slip through your fingers.

River: 10♦-9♣-3♣-7♦-K♠. You hold Q♦-J♣.

Question 10. (a) 10 (b) 1

This scenario is quite different. The king does not appear dangerous to someone holding an already big hand such as a set or a straight. It is likely that your opponents have such holdings and will bet. On your lucky day RisingSun will bet and TheDevil will raise, but whatever happens you should get some action. Betting out cannot be right, as it will just alert these players to the fact that you have made a hand.

Question 11. (a) 0 (b) 0 (c) 5

You've now hit the nuts on the river in consecutive pots. Enjoy it while you can. It won't happen very often.

♣ — ♥ — ♦ — ♠ — ♣ — ♥ — ♦ — ♠

 TIP: Calculating outs with drawing hands is an inexact science. You must be aware of all kinds of holdings that other players may have which can taint your outs. When the other players are telling you, by their strong betting, that they have good hands, you must assess carefully how these can impact on your outs. This is the only way you can accurately assess whether or not you have decent odds for your draw.

Hand 20

Swimming with Sharks

♣ — ♥ — ♦ — ♠ — ♣ — ♥ — ♦ — ♠

INTRODUCTION

This is a short-handed four-player $20-$40 game. There are two weak players in the game, Fish1 and Fish2, and a strong player, SlimJim. The four of you have been tangling for an hour or so and you have done well, focusing your efforts on the river-dwellers and manoeuvring carefully around SlimJim. SlimJim has also made a good profit. Unfortunately, Fish1 has now run out of money and is sitting out, hopefully while he goes off to reload. Fish2 is flush with funds but has also decided to sit out. Naturally you are hoping that he too will soon rejoin the game. SlimJim remains happy to play, and you have been contesting pots with him heads-up for about the last ten minutes.

Before we move on to the hand itself you have a 'pre-play' question.

Question 1. We know that SlimJim is a good player. So, why are you engaging him in this heads-up battle?

(a) I am anxious to keep the game going. The fish may return at any point and then we have a good game again. I am worried that if I sit out, or leave, the game will break up and I will have lost a good chance to continue against the weak players.

(b) I know that SlimJim is strong, but this is a good opportunity for me to hone my skills against a good player. It may cost me some money – or at least I may be playing with a small negative expectation, but I think the learning experience will be good for me.

(c) I have a big ego; I am a strong player and I like to challenge the best. Anyway, I've been watching him play and I am not scared of him.

(d) I have just realised that I have misread his name and I thought I was playing one of the fish. I will sit out after this hand.

| (a) ☐ | (b) ☐ | (c) ☐ | (d) ☐ | Points: .... |

THE PLAY

Online sites vary in the way they handle heads-up play. At this particular site the button is also the big blind. Thus if you are on the small blind you will have to speak first on every round.

For this particular deal you are the button/big blind and you have 5♣-4♣.

Pre-flop

Hypothetical Pre-flop 1

Let's get rid of SlimJim and assume that you are playing heads-up against Fish2. In previous hands when Fish2 was in the small blind, he has never once limped. He has raised with approximately 50% of his hands and folded the others. You have tended to call his raises but have then given up when you missed on the flop. He now raises. There is $60 in the pot and it is $20 to you.

Question 2. Do you (a) fold (b) call (c) raise?

| (a) ☐ | (b) ☐ | (c) ☐ | Points: .... |

Hypothetical Pre-flop 2

Now we are back with SlimJim and the previous play has been exactly as in the first hypothetical question. He now raises. There is $60 in the pot and it is $20 to you.

Question 3. Do you (a) fold (b) call (c) raise?

| (a) ☐ | (b) ☐ | (c) ☐ | Points: .... |

Hypothetical Pre-flop 3

The play is now exactly as in the second hypothetical question with one exception. SlimJim has been raising from his small blind approximately 80% of the time and otherwise folding. You have tended to call his raises but have then given up when you missed on the flop. He now raises yet again. There is $60 in the pot and it is $20 to you.

Question 4. Do you (a) fold (b) call (c) raise?

(a) ☐   (b) ☐   (c) ☐   Points: ....

Actual Pre-flop

In the three previous hands when he had the small blind, SlimJim limped on every occasion. Your hands were as follows (all unsuited): 6-2, 9-3 and 7-3. On each occasion you checked. You now have 5♣-4♣ and SlimJim again limps.

Question 5. Do you (a) check (b) raise?

(a) ☐   (b) ☐   Points: ....

You raise and SlimJim calls.

Flop

Hypothetical Flop

The flop is Q♠-6♣-3♠. You hold 5♣-4♣. SlimJim bets and you raise with your open straight draw. SlimJim now three-bets. There is $180 in the pot and it is $20 to you.

Question 6. Do you (a) fold (b) call (c) cap the pot?

(a) ☐   (b) ☐   (c) ☐   Points: ....

Actual Flop

The flop is again . You hold 5♣-4♣. SlimJim now checks. There is $80 in the pot and it is $20 to you.

Question 7. Do you (a) check (b) bet?

(a) ☐   (b) ☐   Points: ....

You bet and SlimJim now raises. There is $140 in the pot and it is $20 to you.

Question 8. Do you (a) fold (b) call (c) raise?

(a) ☐   (b) ☐   (c) ☐   Points: ....

You raise and SlimJim just calls.

Turn

The turn is Q♠-6♣-3♠-8♥. You hold 5♣-4♣. SlimJim checks. There is $200 in the pot and it is $40 to bet.

Question 9. Do you (a) check (b) bet?

(a) ☐	(b) ☐	Points: ....

You bet and SlimJim calls.

River

Hypothetical River

The river is Q♠-6♣-3♠-8♥-Q♦. You hold 5♣-4♣. Let's assume that you haven't been running on empty (or at least severely depleted) but actually have a hand. You hold A♠-K♠ and the play of the hand has otherwise been exactly the same. Unfortunately, this fine draw has hit blanks. SlimJim now bets. There is $320 in the pot and it is $40 to you.

Question 10. Do you (a) fold (b) call (c) raise?

(a) ☐	(b) ☐	(c) ☐	Points: ....

Actual River

The river is again Q♠ 6♣-3♠-8♥-Q♦. You can now have your 5♣-4♣ back. SlimJim now bets. There is $320 in the pot and it is $40 to you.

Question 11. Do you (a) fold (b) call (c) raise?

(a) ☐	(b) ☐	(c) ☐	Points: ....
			Total: ....

You raise. SlimJim folds quickly. Nice one.

♣ — ♥ — ♦ — ♠ — ♣ — ♥ — ♦ — ♠

SCORECHART

100	Excellent. You are a fearsome heads-up player.
90-99	Very good. You are not afraid to take the initiative.
80-89	Good. You must have played with a decent amount of aggression.
70-79	Average. If you want to try heads-up, stick to small stakes.
60-69	Heads-up play probably does not suit your temperament. However, it is easy enough to stick to full ring play.
below 60	Poor.

♣ – ♥ – ♦ – ♠ – ♣ – ♥ – ♦ – ♠

ANSWERS AND ANALYSIS

Question 1. (a) 0 (b) 0 (c) 8 (d) 20

There are thousands of fish online and you are swimming with the sharks? There is *no* excuse for being involved here.

(a) Okay – it's a good game when the fish are in, and it's not a problem to have a tough player at the table while they are around, but they are *not* around right now. You have no idea whether they are coming back or not. There are thousands of weak players around who you can tangle with – go off and find them. You do not need to waste valuable time playing a game with – at best – no edge. You know that SlimJim is good and for all you know he may be *really* strong heads-up. After all, you are a decent player and he probably realises this, but nevertheless he seems happy enough to play you.

(b) You want to learn? This is admirable, but you don't need to jeopardise your bankroll by tangling with SlimJim to achieve this. You can read books, run simulations, watch good players, read Internet poker forums etc. None of these will cost you money.

(c) You are clearly confident and – up to a point – self-aware. These are good qualities to have as a poker player. However, you are involved in a random online poker game – you are not sitting at the World Series final table with the railbirds hanging on your every move. Wake up and move on.

(d) You are clearly not at your best, but at least you have realised your mistake. If you want to play successful online poker you need to be 100% alert. If you now decide to log off and go to bed you get an extra 10 points.

Holding: 5♣-4♣.

Question 2. (a) 0 (b) 6 (c) 10

The first point here is that you should not fold. When you are playing heads-up normal starting hand values go out of the window. Your 5♣-4♣ is poor, but it is perfectly playable unless Fish2 has a high pair.

There is not a lot wrong with calling. You have position and get to see the flop cheaply. However, playing heads-up is all about taking the initiative, and it is about time you sent a message to Fish2 that he cannot safely raise from the small blind without risking a three-bet. Of course, this play is not remotely justified by your holding, but you do not want him to be able to take the initiative on 50% of the occasions that he is in the small blind. So, three-bet him and bet out on the flop whatever comes. The chances are that his holding is modest, and that he will give up if the flop misses him (which it will more often than not).

Question 3. (a) 0 (b) 10 (c) 7

Again there is no reason to fold. However, when you are playing a tough player there is less to be gained by raising. SlimJim knows about heads-up play and he knows that you will try to take the initiative away from him whenever possible. He will not be cowed by your three-bet in the same way that Fish2 might. He is 'only' raising around 50% of his hands, so he is not trying it on with absolute junk. At some point you must send a message that you won't put up with this forever, but this hand is not the best time to do so. You will get a better opportunity soon enough.

Question 4. (a) 0 (b) 4 (c) 10

SlimJim is stealing your big blinds nearly every time. You *cannot* let him continue to get away with this larceny. You should have made a stand before now and it must not wait any longer. You have a poor hand, but he is raising with 80% of his hands. This means he must be raising it up, out of position, with some real junk. Your passive play to date has been poor, but it is not all bad news. Now that you have finally played back at him, SlimJim will probably put you on a decent hand.

Question 5. (a) 2 (b) 5

The action has been different to previous examples, but the principle is again the same. In Question 4 you had to let SlimJim know that you are not going to tolerate him stealing your big blinds. Now you have to let him know that he cannot get to see endless cheap flops. You have position – so use it to take the initiative.

Flop: Q♠-6♣-3♠. You hold 5♣-4♣.

Question 6. (a) 0 (b) 4 (c) 5

This is a very close decision. Against a weaker player capping the pot would definitely be in order. Against SlimJim the situation is less clear. The point of capping is to keep the initiative, so that if you are both drawing and no-one connects then you can simply bet your opponent out of the pot. However, as SlimJim is strong he will be well aware that your aggressive play may merely signify a decent draw and not a made hand. This is one of the problems of facing strong players, especially short-handed or heads-up. It is much easier to manipulate weaker players as they tend to crawl into a shell when you show strength. Strong players don't.

Question 7. (a) 0 (b) 5

Not much to think about here. You have a minimum of eight outs and must keep the initiative to give yourself a chance of winning without making your hand.

Question 8. (a) 0 (b) 2 (c) 5

By now you should be getting the hang of this. The flop – with precisely one high card – is a classic steal proposition. SlimJim could have absolutely nothing, but he knows that in all probability you have missed the flop, so he is trying to steal it from you. Tell him you have a queen – he may well believe you. Note that the re-raise also sets up the possibility of taking a free card on the turn, although keeping the initiative may well be a preferable strategy – assuming you miss on the turn.

Turn: Q♠-6♣-3♠-8♥. You hold 5♣-4♣.

Question 9. (a) 0 (b) 5

This is not the time to take a free card. You might get check-raised but you have shown a lot of strength and still have your eight outs.

Question 10. (a) 0 (b) 5 (c) 0

SlimJim's bet is rather fishy. It is not impossible that he has a queen, but it smells like he has missed a draw and is hoping – correctly – that you have too. However, you hold the 'high card nuts' and should call. The pot is paying 7-to-1 and a call must have positive expectation. Raising is pointless – SlimJim either has a decent hand or he has a busted draw. He is not going to suddenly bet the river with a pair of threes and then fold to a raise.

River: Q♠-6♣-3♠-8♥-Q♦. You hold 5♣-4♣.

Question 11. (a) 8 (b) 0 (c) 20

Nothing has changed and SlimJim's bet is still fishy. The problem now is that you cannot win by calling. Also, the alert amongst you will have spotted that you cannot win by folding. Thus you must raise and hold your breath. The right way to raise is quickly, but not *too* quickly. An instant raise will be suspicious.

Your bluff raise only has to work 25% of the time to be profitable and, as such, must be a decent try. Note that you should only do this against SlimJim – a known good player who can fold in this situation. It is quite possible that a player such as Fish1 or Fish2 might try SlimJim's river bluff. However, when you raise them, they might get curious and call you with as little as ace-high.

♣ – ♥ – ♦ – ♠ – ♣ – ♥ – ♦ – ♠

TIP: Heads-up play requires a completely different approach to full ring game play. The initiative is everything and you have to compete hard, even with very poor holdings. Heads-up play can be rewarding, but it is not for the faint-hearted. If you do not feel comfortable betting and raising with weak hands then stick to full ring play.

Hand 21

Two Queens

♣ — ♥ — ♦ — ♠ — ♣ — ♥ — ♦ — ♠

INTRODUCTION

This is a full ring ten-player $15-$30 game. You are in the small blind with Q♣-Q♠. This is a reasonable game without being great. The players are typically slightly loose and tend to play their hands in a rather straight-forward fashion. The big blind is Shooter. Shooter is very straightforward indeed. He is solid, bets his hands for value and you have never seen him make any kind of move on anybody. You know where you are with Shooter. The cut-off is VegasPro, who doesn't live up to his name. He is similar to Shooter but is looser pre-flop. Post-flop, VegasPro is interesting. He can play very well and is capable of making plays and also making tough folds. However, he is inconsistent and often struggles due to his loose pre-flop standards. What you have noticed about both players is that they tend to focus too much on their own cards, and not think about what the opposition might hold.

THE PLAY

Pre-flop

It is passed round to LateShift who is in middle position. You are not familiar with LateShift, but the evidence of the play so far suggests that he is a fairly typical player for this game as identified in the introduction. LateShift open-raises, VegasPro calls and the button folds. There is $85 in the pot and it is $30 to you.

Question 1. Do you (a) fold (b) call (c) raise?

| (a) ☐ | (b) ☐ | (c) ☐ | Points: .... |

You raise. Much to your surprise, Shooter now throws $45 in and caps the betting. LateShift calls quickly. VegasPro ponders for a while and eventually calls. There is $225 in the pot and it is $15 to you.

Question 2. Do you (a) fold (b) call?

(a) ☐   (b) ☐   Points: ....

Flop

The flop is 10♦-9♦-4♥. You hold Q♣-Q♠. There is $240 in the pot and it is $15 to bet.

Question 3. Do you (a) check, awaiting developments (b) check, planning a check-raise (c) bet?

(a) ☐   (b) ☐   (c) ☐   Points: ....

You bet. Shooter thinks for a moment and raises.

Hypothetical Play 1

LateShift now three-bets and VegasPro calls the $45 quickly. There is $375 in the pot and it is $30 to you.

Question 4. Do you (a) fold (b) call (c) cap the betting?

(a) ☐   (b) ☐   (c) ☐   Points: ....

Hypothetical Play 2

LateShift folds quickly. VegasPro now three-bets. There is $330 in the pot and it is $30 to you.

Question 5. Which of the following best describes your response?

(a) I am sure I am badly beaten. Fold.

(b) I don't like the look of this, but the pot is now very big. I really have to call here, but I may well release the hand on the turn.

(c) I suspect that VegasPro is drawing, so I will cap to put pressure on Shooter.

(d) I have a big overpair, so I will cap for value.

(a) ☐   (b) ☐   (c) ☐   (d) ☐   Points: ....

Actual Play

LateShift folds quickly. VegasPro thinks for a while and just calls. There is $315 in the pot and it is $15 to you.

Question 6. Do you (a) fold (b) call (c) raise?

(a) ☐	(b) ☐	(c) ☐	Points: ....

You call.

Turn

The turn is 10♦-9♦-4♥-Q♥. You hold Q♣-Q♠. There is $330 in the pot and it is $30 to bet.

Question 7. Do you (a) check, planning a check-raise (b) bet?

(a) ☐	(b) ☐		Points: ....

You check.

Shooter bets quickly and VegasPro instantly raises. There is $420 in the pot and it is $60 to you.

Question 8. Do you (a) fold (b) call (c) raise?

(a) ☐	(b) ☐	(c) ☐	Points: ....

You raise. Shooter now agonises until his time nearly runs out and then calls the $60. VegasPro caps the betting. There is $630 in the pot and it is $30 to you.

Question 9. Do you (a) fold (b) call?

(a) ☐	(b) ☐		Points: ....

You call, as does Shooter.

River

The river is 10♦-9♦-4♥-Q♥-2♦. You hold Q♣-Q♠. There is $690 in the pot and it is $30 to bet.

Question 10. Do you (a) check, planning to call (b) check, hoping to check-raise (c) bet?

(a) ☐	(b) ☐	(c) ☐	Points: ....
			Total: ....

You bet. Both players call and your top set is good. You take down a very nice $780 pot, with 26 big bets in it. The hand history shows that Shooter had K♥-K♠, whereas VegasPro had 9♣-9♥ and flopped a set.

♣ — ♥ — ♦ — ♠ — ♣ — ♥ — ♦ — ♠

SCORECHART

100 — Excellent. Q-Q is hard to handle when you are not sure you have the best hand

90-99 — Very good. Just the right amount of aggression and circumspection.

80-89 — Good. You may have missed a chance or two to push your hand harder.

70-79 — Average.

60-69 — Never mind. You probably got to the river and picked up a nice pot.

below 60 — Poor.

♣ — ♥ — ♦ — ♠ — ♣ — ♥ — ♦ — ♠

ANSWERS AND ANALYSIS

Holding: Q♣-Q♠.

Question 1. (a) 0 (b) 2 (c) 5

It is highly likely that you have the best hand here and you should raise. You want more money in the pot and you don't want to give the big blind a cheap look at the flop. It is possible to call in such a situation, planning to take the initiative if no overcards come on the flop, and players do often like to play like this, especially out of position. Calling also disguises the strength of your holding, and makes it easier to get away from the hand if overcards flop and the opposition get excited. Also, since the pot has already been raised, the big blind may not be along for the ride anyway.

Nevertheless, the simple fact is that you almost certainly have the best hand and you lose a lot of current round equity by failing to raise. The advantages of calling, as detailed above, do not really compensate for this.

Question 2. (a) 0 (b) 5

I do hope you didn't get this one wrong. Shooter's raise is rather worrying though. You have three-bet out of position and the pot has been capped by a very straightforward player. You may very well not have the best hand and must not get carried away if the flop comes with all rags. It is hard to believe that someone like Shooter would cap in such a situation without aces or kings, although it is possible he has A-K suited.

Flop: 10♦-9♦-4♥. You hold Q♣-Q♠.

Question 3. (a) 12 (b) 2 (c) 15

In situations like this you really want to find out what out where you are, and betting offers the best chance to accomplish this. Shooter obviously has a big hand, whilst LateShift and VegasPro have weaker holdings which may or may not have connected with this flop. Shooter is straightforward and, if he has A-A or K-K, he will raise. This will confront LateShift and VegasPro with a double bet and how they respond should give you a good idea of where you are in the hand.

Checking, planning a check-raise, is way over the top. You should be very concerned that your queens are not best, and escalating the pot in this way is just silly. The only circumstances whereby this might be justified would be if Shooter were a tough player who might be capable of folding (not immediately but later in the deal) A-A or K-K, and then you have to hope that your queens stand up against the drawing hands that Late-Shift and/or VegasPro presumably hold. This in itself is a bit of a long shot, but we already know that Shooter is very straightforward and, unless the board becomes horrible, he is not going to be barged out when holding a big overpair.

However, checking and just awaiting developments is a reasonable play. Shooter will obviously bet and if it comes round to you without a further raise you have a decent call for just $15 in this big pot to try and turn a set. If either LateShift or VegasPro raise before the action gets back to you, you should fold. It is absolutely not worth paying $30 when:

1) There is a serious danger that you do not have the best hand.

2) You may run into a re-raise from Shooter (and maybe even further raises after that).

3) You do not have anywhere near pot odds to try and improve your hand.

Taking all this into consideration, I still slightly prefer betting to checking and awaiting developments. The play may have a slight negative expectation, but it has a better chance to clarify where you stand in the hand. The pot is already big and is likely to get much bigger. You do not want to make a mistake in such circumstances, and it is probably worth making a slightly 'inferior' play if it minimises the risk of playing badly later in the hand.

Question 4. (a) 5 (b) 0 (c) 0

Your hand is junk. You are facing two raisers and someone prepared to call three bets cold. The chance of your hand being good is almost nil and the Q♦ (which puts a three-flush on board) is not even a clean out. Someone (probably Shooter) has at least A-A or K-K, and someone else may well have a set. The pot is very big and your pot odds are huge, but none of this helps if your hand is toast and you playing one out.

Question 5. (a) 2 (b) 10 (c) 4 (d) 0

You might be beaten but it is not yet clear that this is the case. VegasPro may well be on a draw and it is not certain that Shooter's hand beats yours, although this is obviously a worry. The pot is just too big for you give up yet.

Capping the pot would be a reasonable play if there was a chance that it would persuade Shooter to fold A-A or K-K, but this is – to say the least – rather unlikely.

Question 6. (a) 0 (b) 10 (c) 2

This is an easy call (you almost have odds to hit your set) and raising is pointless. Calling closes the betting, whereas raising exposes you to a potentially unpleasant re-raise.

Turn: 10♦-9♦-4♥-Q♥. You hold Q♣-Q♠.

Question 7. (a) 10 (b) 2

You have hit your miracle card and there is every chance your hand is now good. Although the Q♥ is an overcard to the flop, if Shooter has A-A or K-K it will only look mildly scary and he will probably bet. Thus this is a good moment to try for a check-raise. The pot is big, VegasPro is very likely to be drawing and it is unlikely that Shooter will check and risk a free card.

Betting out will look suspicious and might encourage Shooter to just call. You might argue that if you bet and Shooter raises then it will make it hard for VegasPro to call with a drawing hand (if he wants to get the right price). However, by that time there will be $420 in the pot and it will be 'only' $60 to VegasPro. He will certainly call with a flush draw and can also call with weaker hands such as J-10 – and he will be right to do so.

When you are winning but your hand is vulnerable, you should instinctively look for a way to protect your hand. Here, however, there is just no way to achieve this. Therefore you should adopt the second best strategy, which is trying to get as much money as possible into the pot and hoping that your hand holds up. The check-raise strategy is the best way to achieve this.

Question 8. (a) 0 (b) 5 (c) 20

Well, VegasPro thinks he is winning. The question is – is he right? He is only winning if he has made a straight and for this to be the case he must be playing either J-8 or K-J. The former of these is wildly improbable, since he initially called two bets cold pre-flop and then called two more when the pot was capped. We know that he is a bit loose, but he is not *that* loose. K-J is possible but even that is very loose pre-flop play. Having K-J also means that he called two bets cold on the flop (risking a further raise) with only a gutshot. VegasPro is a good enough player to realise that his overcards are almost worthless in this situation.

So, what is this hand that he assumes is winning that he was also happy to call a raise with pre-flop? It is most likely to be a lower set, 10-10 or 9-9. He won't have played the hand very well in that case – failing to protect his hand by three-betting the flop, for example – but at least his play would then be logical.

On the balance of probabilities we are winning and must re-raise.

Question 9. (a) 0 (b) 5

Hmm. Maybe he does have K-J after all. Well, we have outs even if he does and a lower set still seems the most likely explanation for his play.

River: 10♦-9♦-4♥-Q♥-2♦. You hold Q♣-Q♠.

Question 10. (a) 5 (b) 2 (c) 15

The third diamond is unlikely to have given anyone a winning hand against you. If Shooter had A♦-K♦, he would not have agonised when calling $60 on the turn. It would have been an easy call, as he would have had numerous outs to the nuts. It is also rather improbable that VegasPro would played the turn as he did with a drawing hand, especially the final cap.

So, the river has probably not changed anything. However, if you check, VegasPro, seeing the three-flush, may get cold feet and just check it down (it is most unlikely that Shooter is going to do any betting). Also, if he is beating you with K-J, he may simply call anyway, frightened that you have drawn him out. A final advantage of betting is that Shooter may well make a crying call.

Thus betting maximises your gains when you are winning and is unlikely to cost anything extra if you are losing.

♣ – ♥ – ♦ – ♠ – ♣ – ♥ – ♦ – ♠

 TIP: It doesn't matter how big or small the pot is, you must try to extract the absolute most from your hand. Even with very big hands players sometimes freeze up when they don't hold the absolute nuts. Here, for example, many players might fail to three-bet the turn, seeing that a straight with K-J (or less likely) J-8 is possible. Also it is possible to check on the river, scared now that a three-flush has materialised. You must always think carefully about what your opponents are *likely* to hold, rather than be scared of what they theoretically might have.

Hand 22

Dead Unlucky

♣ — ♥ — ♦ — ♠ — ♣ — ♥ — ♦ — ♠

INTRODUCTION

This is an eight-player $20-$40 game. You are in the big blind with 6♣-6♠. TheRabbit, a very poor player whom we met in Hand 2, is in middle position. The button is TheMan, an excellent player whom we met in Hand 9.

THE PLAY

Pre-flop

The first two players fold and next to speak is TheRabbit, who limps. The next two players fold and now TheMan raises from the button. The small blind folds and it is up to you.

Hypothetical Plays

I am now going to take away your pair of sixes and substitute some different holdings. What would you do with the following hands?

You have A♣-6♥. There is $90 in the pot and it is $20 to you.

Question 1a. Do you (a) fold (b) call (c) raise?

(a) ☐	(b) ☐	(c) ☐	Points: ....

You have A♣-8♣. There is $90 in the pot and it is $20 to you.

Question 1b. Do you (a) fold (b) call (c) raise?

(a) ☐	(b) ☐	(c) ☐	Points: ....

You have 9♥-9♣. There is $90 in the pot and it is $20 to you.

Question 1c. Do you (a) fold (b) call (c) raise?

(a) ☐   (b) ☐   (c) ☐   Points: ....

You have 8♥-7♦. There is $90 in the pot and it is $20 to you.

Question 1d. Do you (a) fold (b) call (c) raise?

(a) ☐   (b) ☐   (c) ☐   Points: ....

Actual Play

We now return to your actual holding of 6♣-6♠. There is $90 in the pot and it is $20 to you.

Question 2. Do you (a) fold (b) call (c) raise?

(a) ☐   (b) ☐   (c) ☐   Points: ....

You call, as does TheRabbit

Flop

Hypothetical Play

The flop is 8♦-6♥-6♦ and you hold 6♣-6♠. Well, lucky you – you have flopped quads. If you play a pair pre-flop this is a 407-to-1 shot, so it will happen now and again.

We will now get rid of TheMan for the moment and substitute MrFish who, as you may have guessed, is a weak player, much along the lines of MrRabbit. The pre-flop play is exactly the same. There is $130 in the pot and it is $20 to bet.

Question 3. Do you (a) check, planning to call (b) check, planning a check-raise (c) bet?

(a) ☐   (b) ☐   (c) ☐   Points: ....

Actual Play

The flop is 8♦-6♥-6♦. You hold 6♣-6♠. The bad news is that MrFish has gone fishing and we are now back with TheMan on the button. The good news is that you have flopped quads and, barring a miracle, the pot is yours. There is $130 in the pot and it is $20 to bet.

Question 4. Do you (a) check, planning to call (b) check, planning a check-raise (c) bet?

(a) ☐	(b) ☐	(c) ☐	Points: ....

You bet. MrRabbit now calls and TheMan raises. There is $210 in the pot and it is $20 to you.

Question 5. Do you (a) fold (b) call (c) raise?

(a) ☐	(b) ☐	(c) ☐	Points: ....

You call, as does TheRabbit.

Turn

The turn is 8♦-6♥-6♦-4♦. You hold 6♣-6♠. There is $250 in the pot and it is $40 to bet.

Question 6. Do you (a) check (b) bet?

(a) ☐	(b) ☐	Points: ....

You bet. TheRabbit calls quickly. TheMan now raises. There is $410 in the pot and it is $40 to you.

Question 7. Do you (a) fold (b) call (c) raise?

(a) ☐	(b) ☐	(c) ☐	Points: ....

You raise. TheRabbit now has a long think but eventually calls. TheMan also calls.

River

The river is 8♦-6♥-6♦-4♦-K♣. You hold 6♣-6♠. There is $610 in the pot and it is $40 to bet.

Question 8. Do you (a) check (b) bet?

(a) ☐	(b) ☐	Points: ....
		Total: ....

You bet, TheRabbit folds and TheMan calls. The hand history shows that he had K♦-Q♦.

I feel a little sorry for TheMan in this pot. His play puts me in mind of Bruce Willis in *The Sixth Sense*. He is running around, doing all the usual stuff – raising with position and a decent hand, raising with a strong draw, raising for value ... the only problem is ... he is dead the whole time – he just didn't know it. At least this is only poker – Bruce Willis' character really was dead.

♣ – ♥ – ♦ – ♠ – ♣ – ♥ – ♦ – ♠

SCORECHART

100	Excellent. You focused very well on your opponents and made the most of your good fortune.
90-99	Very good. You handle quads excellently. Let's hope you hit them more often than once in every 408 times you see the flop with a pair.
80-89	Good. However, you may have failed to extract an extra bet or two.
70-79	Average. Concentrate with any hand. Even when there is no danger of losing.
60-69	Never mind. At least you hit a big flop. Maybe you are hot and can do it again.
below 60	Poor.

♣ – ♥ – ♦ – ♠ – ♣ – ♥ – ♦ – ♠

ANSWERS AND ANALYSIS

Question 1a. (a) 5 (b) 2 (c) 0

You can assume that TheRabbit will call and so your pot odds are 5½-to-1. However, you only have a feeble ace and this is just not worth it. It is very likely that your hand is dominated by TheMan, either with a decent pair or a stronger ace and even TheRabbit may well have a hand that dominates yours. The trouble with these Ace-junk hands is that it is very hard to make any money with them. If an ace flops and you are winning you are not likely to get paid off, whereas if you are losing you may well feel obliged to go to the river. The only real chance to score with a hand like this is to hit an unlikely two pair, and even these hands are vulnerable to a player with a stronger ace, since they will always have a reasonable number of outs against you; a late running pair (higher than sixes) will always counterfeit your second pair. Note that having A-6 you cannot even hope for an unlikely low straight – at least not using both of your cards.

Question 1b. (a) 3 (b) 5 (c) 0

This is a much more playable hand. You are suited and your side card has improved. You can now call, but as usual you have to play the hand well and not get carried away even if you make a pair on the flop.

Question 1c. (a) 0 (b) 4 (c) 10

Your 9-9 is quite a strong holding here and it would be good to get TheRabbit out. A pair of nines has a much better chance to win unimproved when playing heads up rather than in a three player pot. The most likely holding for TheMan is two overcards to your nines when chances are approximately 50/50. However, he might well have a weaker hand and then you would be in very good shape. In any event, removing TheRabbit from the scene would certainly improve your pot equity, and by forcing him to put $40 into a $130 pot, you may achieve this. Many players will just call here, hoping that the flop comes low. However, re-raising is a much better play.

Question 1d. (a) 5 (b) 3 (c) 0

I am inclined to dump this one. 8-7 offsuit is really just too weak to pay a whole small bet even with reasonable pot odds. If you throw another couple of callers in and you pot odds are getting close to 9-to-1 or 10-to1 then it is reasonable to call, but you only have 5½-to1 and this is not good value.

Holding: 6♣-6♠.

Question 2. (a) 0 (b) 5 (c) 0

This is an easy call and any other play is poor. You have a good chance to get paid off if you hit your set and if rags pop up all over the place then your 6-6 may well hold up unimproved.

Question 3. (a) 10 (b) 4 (c) 4

This is a perfect moment to slowplay and a check-call, allowing the opposition the chance to improve on the turn is the best way to do this. You have two weak opponents and they are not the kind of players who will make plays with overcards or draws. If you show strength to such players they tend to give up with nothing or just call with moderate hands. They will only get aggressive if they really have something decent. With the current state of the board this is unlikely and you should give them the chance to make a hand. If you bet now or check-raise, they may dump their hands straight away.

Flop: 8♦-6♥-6♦. You hold 6♣-6♠.

Question 4. (a) 10 (b) 4 (c) 20

Now that we have a decent aggressive player at the table a bet is much more likely to build the pot than a slowplay. The trouble with checking is that TheRabbit will check and TheMan will bet. Now all we can do to get more money into the pot is check-raise, but this is likely to get rid of TheRabbit, which is the last thing we want to do.

Question 5. (a) 0 (b) 10 (c) 2

As planned. You don't want to raise here, since you would like to keep TheRabbit in the pot. It is unlikely that anyone has much of a hand yet but, with a two-flush and two reasonably connected cards, there are decent drawing possibilities.

Turn: 8♦-6♥-6♦-4♦. You hold 6♣-6♠.

Question 6. (a) 2 (b) 10

This is an excellent card for you. The flush draw has made it whilst anyone with A♦ is going to hang around for the river, not realising that they are drawing dead. Betting again has a much better chance of building the pot than checking – for more or less the same reasons as given in the answer to Question 4.

Question 7. (a) 0 (b) 2 (c) 15

There is no point messing around any longer. The pot is now very big and TheRabbit is a soft, loose player who will probably call the two bets even with quite a poor holding. You never know – someone may even have 8-8 and give you unlimited action. Calling is a very poor play – you will definitely maximise your expectation by raising.

River: 8♦-6♥-6♦-4♦-K♣. You hold 6♣-6♠.

Question 8. (a) 0 (b) 5

No-one is going to bet the river for you.

♣ — ♥ — ♦ — ♠ — ♣ — ♥ — ♦ — ♠

 Tip: It is easy to got complacent when you flop an unbeatable hand. You know that you are going to win the pot, so there is a temptation to just relax and enjoying it. Fight this. Extra bets that you can extract from the opposition here are just as important as extra bets you win by sophisticated plays with more modest holdings.

Hand 23

Applying Pressure

♣ — ♥ — ♦ — ♠ — ♣ — ♥ — ♦ — ♠

INTRODUCTION

This is an eight-player $20-$40 game. You are in the big blind with 10♥-8♥. Yet again you are pleased to be sitting at the same table as TheRabbit, a very poor player who we met in Hands 2 and 22. TheRabbit is in middle position. The button is Cyprus. You know Cyprus well – he is a competent, aggressive player but no world-beater. He is typical of many reasonable players in that he bets his hard pre-flop and on the flop but tends to play more conservatively on the turn and river.

THE PLAY

Pre-flop

The first two players fold and next to speak is TheRabbit, who limps. The next two players fold and now Cyprus raises from the button. The small blind folds. There is $90 in the pot and it is $20 to you.

Question 1. Do you (a) fold (b) call (c) raise?

(a) ☐   (b) ☐   (c) ☐   Points: ....

You call, as does TheRabbit.

Flop

Hypothetical Flop

The flop is 10♦-8♣-6♦. You hold 10♥-8♥. There is $130 in the pot and it is $20 to bet.

162

Question 2. Do you (a) check, planning to call (b) check, planning a check-raise (c) bet?

(a) ☐	(b) ☐	(c) ☐	Points: ....

Actual Flop

The flop is 9♦-6♥-2♣. You hold 10♥-8♥. There is $130 in the pot and it is $20 to bet.

Question 3. Do you (a) check, planning to call (b) check, planning a check raise (c) bet?

(a) ☐	(b) ☐	(c) ☐	Points: ....

You check, TheRabbit checks and Cyprus bets. There is $150 in the pot and it is $20 to you.

Question 4. Do you (a) fold (b) call (c) raise?

(a) ☐	(b) ☐	(c) ☐	Points: ....

You raise and TheRabbit folds. Cyprus calls.

Turn

Hypothetical Turn 1

The turn is 9♦-6♥-2♣-5♠. You hold 10♥-8♥. There is $210 in the pot and it is $40 to bet.

Question 5. Do you (a) check (b) bet?

(a) ☐	(b) ☐	Points: ....

Hypothetical Turn 2

The turn is 9♦-6♥-2♣-A♠. You hold 10♥-8♥. There is $210 in the pot and it is $40 to bet.

Question 6. Do you (a) check (b) bet?

(a) ☐	(b) ☐	Points: ....

You bet.

Hypothetical Turn 2 continued

Cyprus now raises. You know Cyprus well enough to be 'certain' that he has at least an ace. You also know that you will not be able to push him out of the pot by re-raising. Therefore your only consideration is whether you have a worthwhile call to improve to a winning hand. With this in mind: there is $330 in the pot and it is $40 to you.

Firstly, considering only pot odds:

Question 7a. Do you (a) have a clear fold (b) have a clear call (c) it is a very close decision?

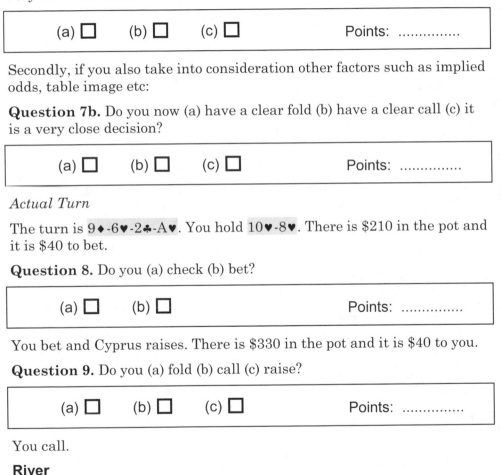

(a) ☐   (b) ☐   (c) ☐   Points: ....

Secondly, if you also take into consideration other factors such as implied odds, table image etc:

Question 7b. Do you now (a) have a clear fold (b) have a clear call (c) it is a very close decision?

(a) ☐   (b) ☐   (c) ☐   Points: ....

Actual Turn

The turn is 9♦-6♥-2♣-A♥. You hold 10♥-8♥. There is $210 in the pot and it is $40 to bet.

Question 8. Do you (a) check (b) bet?

(a) ☐   (b) ☐   Points: ....

You bet and Cyprus raises. There is $330 in the pot and it is $40 to you.

Question 9. Do you (a) fold (b) call (c) raise?

(a) ☐   (b) ☐   (c) ☐   Points: ....

You call.

River

The river is 9♦-6♥-2♣-A♥-9♥. You hold 10♥-8♥. There is $370 in the pot and it is $40 to bet.

Question 10. Do you (a) check (b) bet?

(a) ☐	(b) ☐	Points: ....

You bet. Cyprus now raises. There is $490 in the pot and it is $40 to you.

Question 11. Do you (a) fold (b) call (c) raise?

(a) ☐	(b) ☐	(c) ☐	Points: ....
			Total: ....

You call. Cyprus shows down 6♣-6♦ for a full house.

♣ — ♥ — ♦ — ♠ — ♣ — ♥ — ♦ — ♠

SCORECHART

100	Outstanding. You played excellent hold'em and lost a bundle. This happens all too often.
90-99	Excellent. You have a good feel for when to apply pressure.
80-89	Good. You must have broadly taken the initiative in the right places.
70-79	Average.
60-69	Never mind. Maybe you check-folded early and saved yourself some grief.
below 60	Poor.

♣ — ♥ — ♦ — ♠ — ♣ — ♥ — ♦ — ♠

ANSWERS AND ANALYSIS

Holding: 10♥-8♥.

Question 1. (a) 2 (b) 5 (c) 0

This hand is certainly playable. Had the action so far been different with a raise coming from an early player, and then a call from a late player then it would not be so clear. There would be a greater danger of facing an overpair when you would need to hit the flop hard to have any chance in the pot. In those circumstances a fold is probably best. However, although you can presume that Cyprus has a reasonable holding, there is no need to put him on a powerhouse. He has prime position and is raising a weak player; he could make such a play with a wide variety of hands.

Question 2. (a) 5 (b) 12 (c) 20

Obviously this is a great flop for you as you have hit top two pair. However, your hand is more vulnerable than you may think, especially with TheRabbit having limped into the pot. There are a number of unpleasant cards that can come on the turn: any diamond completes a flush draw, a 9 or 7 complete a potential gutshot and even a 6 will seriously diminish your holding, since you are then losing to a 6 or an overpair and are suddenly vulnerable to overcards. This is no time to be slowplaying your holding, so check-calling – as a slowplay – is horrible.

Nevertheless, check-calling here is a mistake that many players make and so it is worth discussing why this is such a bad play. What they plan to do is check-call the flop and then go for a check-raise on the turn when the bet size doubles. However, if you can visualise how the hand is likely to develop, you can see that there are many problems with this approach:

1) If Cyprus has just overcards, say A-J, and has no drawing possibilities, then the flop will look rather scary for him and he may just check and take the free card. We know that he is aggressive but he is not stupid. He will be well aware that such a flop could easily have connected with the (limping) opposition, and he could decide that he would rather take a free card – trying to hit an overcard – than bet and risk a nasty check-raise. We have already noted how many bad cards can come on the turn so this is a no time to give a free card.

2) However, let's assume Cyprus does bet and you now just call. It is likely that TheRabbit will call too. Now what will you do on the turn? If a bad card comes (e.g. a diamond, a 9 or a 7) will you bet? You probably will because now you cannot play for a check-raise on the turn, since someone may have completed their draw and you could be playing only four outs. So you will probably bet and if you get raised it will be ugly.

However, even if a good card (e.g. a random low card) comes, it is still not clear how you should play the hand. Checking, trying for a check-raise, is dangerous because the hand could easily get checked around. This would be a truly awful outcome – you will have allowed both opponents to get from the flop to the river for a mere $20 apiece. However, if you now bet on the blank card it will look rather suspicious and your opponents are unlikely to give you much action, even with decent hands.

It should be clear from this that you can get into a tangle by check-calling the flop. The main reason is that you are out of position. Such a play becomes more defensible when you have position on the opposition.

Thus the choice is between trying for a check-raise and betting out. The most obvious play is to go for a check-raise. If you check, TheRabbit is likely to check and then Cyprus will probably bet, allowing you to check-raise and put pressure on TheRabbit. This is a reasonable plan but, as we saw above, it cannot be taken for granted that Cyprus will bet. Even if this was the only consideration here it should tip the balance in favour of betting out.

However, there is a further point. If you bet the flop, TheRabbit will probably call. Since Cyprus is aggressive, there is a chance that he may now raise. Indeed, if he has made a half decent hand or hit some kind of draw then this is likely. Now, of course, you re-raise, which achieves the same goal as playing for a check-raise in the first place but now you have encouraged everyone to put an additional $20 in the pot. Since you are almost certainly winning at this point, this is good news.

Betting out is the optimal play. It puts the most pressure on the opposition and creates the best chance to build the pot.

Flop: 9♦-6♥-2♣. You hold 10♥-8♥.

Question 3. (a) 5 (b) 25 (c) 15

This is a very reasonable flop for you. You have a gutshot, an overcard and a backdoor flush draw. This may not sound like much, but you only have two opponents, and no reason to think that either of them has a decent hand, or that they have connected with this raggedy flop.

When you have such a reasonable hand and the flop is unthreatening, check-calling becomes awful play and the choice is between betting and check-raising. You must now think about what your priorities are and which play will create the best chance to achieve them. Your objective here is simple: you want to get players out of the pot – preferably all of them. You need to give yourself a chance to win without making a hand, so you must get aggressive.

If you bet, what will probably happen is that MrRabbit will call with more or less anything. If Cyprus also calls then your bet has not achieved anything, and if a random overcard comes it is going to be hard for you play the hand accurately. It is also possible that Cyprus will raise in this situation. With a couple of good overcards this would be a natural play to create the possibility of a free card on the turn.

This scenario is also unattractive because you will probably have to just call and thus fall in with his plans. You could three-bet to put pressure on TheRabbit, but such a play is fraught with danger. You would be escalating the pot and tying players to their hands when you hold only a modest draw. Your chances of winning without showing down the best hand are then very small, and you have thus deprived yourself of a key component of your strategy.

Checking is much better. TheRabbit will probably check and Cyprus will bet (it will be most surprising if he doesn't – but even that would be no disaster as you then get a free card with your drawing hand). After Cyprus bets, you can raise and put a great deal of pressure on TheRabbit. He will now be facing a $40 call to stay in a $190 pot, and even he will probably fold unless he really has connected properly with the flop.

Note also that by check-raising, you are strongly representing a 9. It is perfectly possible that Cyprus has just overcards. If you can get him heads-up on the turn and a blank comes, he is likely to give up if he cannot beat a pair of nines at that stage.

It is interesting to compare the answer here to that in Question 2. There you had made a very strong hand and the best play was to bet out. Here you have a much weaker hand and yet the best plan is to go for the stronger play of the check-raise! Decisions in hold'em are not formulaic. You should not automatically make a strong play with a strong hand and a modest play with a modest hand. You constantly need to think about what you are trying to achieve and to anticipate how the pot may develop.

Question 4. (a) 1 (b) 0 (c) 5

As planned. You have enough hand to call but raising is a far better play.

Question 5. (a) 0 (b) 5

You absolutely must bet here. If Cyprus has just overcards he will probably fold. He will find it hard to believe that you do not have at least a pair here and is unlikely to invest $80 ($40 now and $40 on the river) to find out.

Question 6. (a) 2 (b) 5

Of course the A♠ is a horrible card for you, but you must grit your teeth and bet. It is possible that this card has not helped your opponent as he might have a low pair or two high cards not including an ace. If that is the case he is likely to fold, and you will have stolen the pot.

Question 7a. (a) 5 (b) 0 (c) 0

Cyprus has a pair of aces or a hand that is even better and thus we need a 7 – completing our straight – to win. We can see six cards and can reasonably assume that Cyprus does not have a 7 in his hand. Therefore we have four winning cards from the remaining pack (44 cards) and we need the pot to be paying us 10-to-1 in order for this to be a worthwhile call. There is currently $330 in the pot and it will cost us $40 to see the river. This is only slightly better than 8-to-1 and so, purely considering pot odds, this is a clear fold.

Question 7b. (a) 6 (b) 6 (c) 10

When we take other factors into consideration, the decision becomes much less clear.

1) If we do hit the miracle 7, the implied odds are rather good. We will probably be able to check-raise the river and gain a further $80. If we could guarantee this, we would be getting $410 ($330 in the pot plus two further big bets on the river) for a $40 investment at pot odds of 10-to-1. This actually makes the play very slightly profitable.

2) If we do draw out horribly on Cyprus he may, with a bit of luck, get annoyed – to the detriment of his future play.

3) We have shown a great deal of aggression in this pot. Calling now, rather than folding, will send a message to Cyprus – plus anyone else who happens to be paying attention – that we cannot easily be pushed out of pots. However, this factor has more relevance in live rather than online play. Players who play online are often playing more than one game or are otherwise distracted, and also move easily from game to game. Thus cultivating an 'image' is less important online.

4) There are very few players – even very good ones – who play an equally good game of poker whether they are winning or losing. Virtually everybody plays at least slightly better with a healthy stack, a good run of cards and some decent pots under their belt. When things are not running for you, it can be difficult to resist the temptation to loosen up in an attempt to recoup your losses. Thus it can be worth making an occasional 'bad' play to give you the chance of a lucky outdraw which may well improve your mood and help you to play better. Note, however, that such a play should only ever be 'slightly' bad.

In this particular example it would be reasonable to assume that you will always gain one further big bet on the river when you hit your 7. Thus you are risking $40 to win $370 with 10-to-1 pot odds. If this scenario is repeated 11 times, you will win once and gain $370 and lose ten times and for a total loss of $400. Thus, your negative expectation on the play is slightly less than $3 ($30 divided by the 11 times the scenario is played out). This is only one-tenth of a big bet and is thus quite reasonable. If the amount were to approach half a big bet then it is becoming a seriously bad play and you should look for other ways to improve your mood.

Turn: 9♦-6♥-2♣-A♥. You hold 10♥-8♥.

Question 8. (a) 0 (b) 5

Compared to Question 7, betting is now an easy decision. You have picked up a further eight outs with the flush draw, but it would still be very good news if your bet persuaded Cyprus to give up.

Question 9. (a) 0 (b) 5 (c) 0

We already know that we cannot push Cyprus out of the pot but, having picked up the flush draw, we no longer need to make pot odds calculations.

River: 9♦-6♥-2♣-A♥-9♥. You hold 10♥-8♥.

Question 10. (a) 1 (b) 5

The 9♥ is a scary card for Cyprus – not just because he will fear a flush but because you represented a 9 with your raise on the flop. He will thus be worried that you have outdrawn him (as indeed it appears you have), and may well take the free showdown. You will then have let a bet slip through your fingers.

Question 11. (a) 0 (b) 5 (c) 0

Raise?? Oh dear. It is perfectly possible that you have a 9 in *your* hand and yet Cyprus doesn't care. Presumably he can beat trip nines and – if he can beat trip nines – he can almost certainly beat your flush. He may have A-9 or he may have flopped a set. However, the pot is huge and folding is absurd. Call, but don't hold your breath.

♣ — ♥ — ♦ — ♠ — ♣ — ♥ — ♦ — ♠

TIP: When you have a modest-sized pot, with only one or two opponents and the board does not look threatening, then it is usually right to make a play for the pot with any half-decent hand. You may take down the pot straight away or set yourself up for a steal later in the hand. The combined chances of stealing the pot and actually making a winning hand are often sufficient for this to be a profitable play.

Hand 24

Telling Tales

♣ — ♥ — ♦ — ♠ — ♣ — ♥ — ♦ — ♠

INTRODUCTION

For this 'hand' I am going to dispense with the standard format for this book, and instead offer puzzles which relate to various themes that can crop up in online play, and online tells in particular.

Hand 1

You are playing in a good ten-player $20-$40 game with loose players who are mostly calling and paying off too much. You are not really involved in this hand, but observe the following scenario played out between RockyHorror and HumblePie. You don't know much about either player, but HumblePie seems absolutely typical of the players in this game. RockyHorror appears to be a little better and is certainly more aggressive, but he is definitely loose. He has been running badly and has, quite quickly, drifted down from $1,000 to about $400.

RockyHorror open-raises from middle position and HumblePie, sitting immediately to his left, calls. You are next and fold, as indeed does everyone else. The flop comes down A♥-9♣-5♠. RockyHorror bets and HumblePie calls. The turn brings A♥-9♣-5♠-2♠. RockyHorror bets again, and HumblePie thinks for a moment and then calls. The river brings A♥-9♣-5♠-2♠-6♥. RockyHorror bets, HumblePie raises and RockyHorror makes a crying call only to be shown 7♦-8♦ for a gutshot straight. RockyHorror flashes his A-K before it hits the muck, and the following educational exchange ensues in the chat box.

    RockyHorror: man, u suck.

    HumblePie: what?

RockyHorror: how can u call with that trash?

HumblePie: I had a gutshot

RockyHorror: idiot. u are a fish

The next hand is dealt and you are in the cut-off seat with A♠-J♦.

Hypothetical Play 1

Assume that the previous hand as described had not taken place, and that the two players who have entered the pot are completely unknown to you. You do not know if they are strong/weak loose/tight etc. It is passed around to RockyHorror, who open-raises, and HumblePie again calls. There is $110 in the pot and it is $40 to you.

Question 1. Do you (a) fold (b) call (c) raise?

(a) ☐   (b) ☐   (c) ☐   Points: ....

Actual Play

We are back with RockyHorror and HumblePie and their happy banter. The action is the same: RockyHorror open-raises, and HumblePie calls. There is $110 in the pot and it is $40 to you.

Question 2. Do you (a) fold (b) call (c) raise?

(a) ☐   (b) ☐   (c) ☐   Points: ....

Hypothetical Play 2

This time RockyHorror open-raises and HumblePie makes it three bets. There is $130 in the pot and it is $60 to you.

Question 3. Do you (a) fold (b) call (c) raise?

(a) ☐   (b) ☐   (c) ☐   Points: ....

Hand 2

You are playing a six-player $15-$30 game. You are in the big blind with 10♥-10♣. Headstrong, a tricky, aggressive player in middle position open-raises. It is passed around to you. Raising is clearly an option but, out of position against a tricky opponent, you decide to call and see the flop. The flop is 8♥-6♣-2♣. You check, and then check-raise when Headstrong inevitably bets. Headstrong now three-bets instantly, and you decide just to call. The turn is 8♥-6♣-2♣-Q♥. You check.

Hypothetical Play

Headstrong now bets instantly. There is $190 in the pot and it is $30 to you.

Question 4. Do you (a) fold (b) call (c) raise?

(a) ☐   (b) ☐   (c) ☐   Points: ....

Actual Play

Headstrong now thinks for a long time almost using up the time allowance, but eventually bets. There is $190 in the pot and it is $30 to you.

Question 5. Do you (a) fold (b) call (c) raise?

(a) ☐   (b) ☐   (c) ☐   Points: ....

Hand 3

You have just joined an eight-player $20-$40 game and posted a late blind in the cut-off position. You are familiar with most of the players in this game. They are typically fairly solid and predictable. Gambit is in the big blind and you have noticed that he is also playing on two other tables. He is a tricky player.

You are dealt 6♣-4♣. It is passed around to Texas, who limps from middle position. You check. Boris, the small blind, throws in $10 and Gambit, in the big blind, checks instantly. Four of you see the flop, which comes down K♥-8♣-3♠. You hold 6♣-4♣. Boris now hesitates for a while but checks.

Hypothetical Play

Gambit thinks for a moment and also checks. Texas then checks fairly quickly. There is $80 in the pot and it is $20 to bet.

Question 6. Do you (a) check (b) bet?

(a) ☐   (b) ☐   Points: ....

Actual Play

Gambit checks instantly, suggesting he has pre-activated his check/fold button. Texas also checks fairly quickly. There is $80 in the pot and it is $20 to you.

Question 7. Do you (a) check (b) bet?

(a) ☐   (b) ☐   Points: ....

Total: ....

♣ — ♥ — ♦ — ♠ — ♣ — ♥ — ♦ — ♠

SCORECHART

100   Excellent. You are very in tune with online play.

90-99   Very good. Don't bother with Vegas – stay at home and play in your pyjamas.

80-89   Good. These online tells can make a difference and you are aware of them.

70-79   Perhaps you prefer live play. This is no bad thing.

60-69   Maybe you surf while you play. Don't. Concentrate on the game.

below 60 Poor.

♣ — ♥ — ♦ — ♠ — ♣ — ♥ — ♦ — ♠

ANSWERS AND ANALYSIS

Question 1. (a) 10 (b) 2 (c) 4

On merit you ought not to have the best hand, so it is best to fold. If you were facing just a raise from middle position, then entering the pot would have some merit. However, you are facing a raise *and* a call and that is a different proposition entirely. Some players will open-raise with the tiniest encouragement, at which point it can be profitable to take them on with a hand such as A♠-J♦. However, you don't know for sure that RockyHorror is such a player and, furthermore, HumblePie has called two bets cold. It is best to fold.

Question 2. (a) 12 (b) 15 (c) 25

These two have gone to war, and you can profit from their battle. Rocky-Horror is fuming at his bad beat and has very likely opened light. Although RockyHorror's chat box exchanges were deplorable, he was right about one thing – HumblePie is indeed a fish. He has probably called – as he did on the previous hand – with a highly inadequate holding. There is a very decent chance that you have the best hand – and you have position.

On merit your hand is not worth playing, but taking into account the state of mind and general ability of these two players, it is worth getting involved. Once you have decided to play, a raise is the best option. If you just call, then the blinds are getting good odds to see the flop with all sorts of holdings, and their participation will certainly weaken your equity in the pot. However, if you raise it is going to cost them an extra bet, and there is a better chance of being able to lever them out.

You are taking something of a risk here. It could be that either Rocky-Horror or HumblePie has picked up a biggie, and that you are struggling with your A-J. However, you are a good player so you are going to play the hand well and release it if you smell trouble.

Question 3. (a) 15 (b) 2 (c) 0

HumblePie raising makes all the difference, and your hand is now a clear fold. HumblePie gives every indication of being a soft, passive player, and when this species three-bets an aggressive opponent, you need an absolute premium hand to compete. You don't have one. Fold.

Question 4. (a) 6 (b) 10 (c) 2

It is very hard to know what to do here, but I would be slightly inclined towards calling HeadStrong down. He would three-bet with a wide range of hands, and the queen will likely only help A-Q and K-Q. All this instant betting is typical of an aggressive player on a flush draw who is trying to force you out of the pot.

Question 5. (a) 8 (b) 10 (c) 2

Playing online, you can never be completely sure why someone has delayed in making their bet. There may be some perfectly innocent explanation such as an unreliable internet connection, unexpected phone call or suddenly screaming baby. However, if they are deliberately delaying, it is very likely that they want you to think that they are weak. The delay would suggest to me that they are actually rather strong, and this would make me slightly more inclined to fold.

Nevertheless, I am sure that the correct poker decision here is to call them down, and ultimately, unless you are totally sure of your read on somebody, you should make the correct poker decision. The point of this example is to alert you to the fact that there can be quite subtle tells in online play, and you should be aware of them, even if they don't affect your immediate decision.

Question 6. (a) 15 (b) 10

A bet, as a complete bluff, is not bad here, but you have three opponents, one of them a tricky player who may well have checked a reasonable hand. Checking is probably more circumspect.

Question 7. (a) 6 (b) 15

You can now be fairly sure that Gambit has no interest whatsoever in this pot and is just waiting to fold while he concentrates on his affairs elsewhere. This means that you have only two straightforward opponents, and now a bet must have a positive expectation. Once you can see that the only tricky opponent is not a threat, it is quite poor play not to take a shot at stealing with 4-to-1 pot odds.

♣ — ♥ — ♦ — ♠ — ♣ — ♥ — ♦ — ♠

TIP: You may notice that the 'wrong' answers in these puzzles are awarded scores that are closer to the 'correct' answers than in many of the other puzzles in this book. This is quite deliberate. Being aware of online tells and mannerisms can only generate a small edge, and making the correct poker decisions is far more important. Nevertheless, every little edge can help your bankroll, so you should be aware of them.

Odds Tables

♣ — ♥ — ♦ — ♠ — ♣ — ♥ — ♦ — ♠

The following tables give useful information about probabilities of improvement and the relative merits of starting hands. This information is reproduced by permission from www.pokerupdate.com, and is Copyright © 2003 Andrew Kinsman.

Starting Hands

The probability of being dealt:

Pocket aces **220/1 (0.45%)**
Any pocket pair **16/1 (5.9%)**

A-K suited **331/1 (0.3%)**
A-K offsuit **110/1 (0.9%)**
A-K suited or offsuit **82/1 (1.2%)**

Any two suited cards **3.3/1 (24%)**
Max stretch suited connectors, e.g. J-T suited **46/1 (2.1%)**
Max stretch connectors, e.g. J-T suited or offsuit **11/1 (8.5%)**

Either pocket aces or pocket kings **110/1 (0.9%)**
Either pocket aces, pocket kings or A-K **46/1 (2.1%)**
Either pocket aces, pocket kings, pocket queens, A-K, A-Q or K-Q **19/1 (5%)**
Any pocket pair or two cards ten or higher **4.5/1 (18%)**
Any pocket pair of sevens or higher or two cards ten or higher **5.4/1 (16%)**

If you take a pocket pair to the river, you have a **4.2/1 (19%)** chance of making a set or better.

If you take two suited cards to the river, you have a **15/1 (6.4%)** chance of making a flush in your suit by then. Your chance of making a flush in your suit by the river with two unsuited cards is **53/1 (1.8%)**.

♣ — ♥ — ♦ — ♠ — ♣ — ♥ — ♦ — ♠

The Flop

The probability of improving to:

A set or better from a pocket pair **7.5/1 (11.8%)**, which is broken down as follows:

A set **8.3/1 (10.8%)**
A full house **136/1 (0.74%)**
Quads **407/1 (0.25%)**

A flush from two suited cards **118/1 (0.84%)**
A four-flush from two suited cards **8.1/1 (10.9%)**
A three-flush from two suited cards **1.4/1 (41.6%)**
A four-flush from one suited card **88/1 (1.1%)**
A three-flush from one suited card **6.8/1 (12.8%)**

A straight from two max stretch connectors **76/1 (1.3%)**
An eight outs (open-ended or double belly buster) straight draw from two max stretch connectors **8.6/1 (10.5%)**
A gutshot straight draw from two max stretch connectors **3.6/1 (22%)**

At least a pair (using pocket cards) from two non-pair cards **2.1/1 (32.4%)**
A pair (using one pocket card) from two non-pair cards **2.5/1 (29%)**
Two pair (using both pocket cards) from two non-pair cards **49/1 (2%)**
Any two pair from two non-pair cards **24/1 (4%)**
Trips (using one of pocket card) from two non-pair cards **73/1 (1.35%)**
A full house (using both pocket cards) from two non-pair cards **1087/1 (0.09%)**
Quads (using one pocket cards) from two non-pair cards **9799/1 (0.01%)**

♣ — ♥ — ♦ — ♠ — ♣ — ♥ — ♦ — ♠

What will appear on the Three Flop Cards

Three of a kind **424/1 (0.24%)**
A pair **5/1 (17%)**
Three suited cards **18/1 (5.2%)**
Two suited cards **0.8/1 (55%)**
No suited cards (rainbow) **1.5/1 (40%)**
Three cards in sequence **28/1 (3.5%)**
Two cards in sequence **1.5/1 (40%)**
No cards in sequence **0.8/1 (56%)**

♣ — ♥ — ♦ — ♠ — ♣ — ♥ — ♦ — ♠

From Flop to Turn

The probability of improving to:

A full house or better from a set on the next card (7 outs) **5.7/1 (15%)**
A full house from two pair on the next card (4 outs) **11/1 (9%)**
A set from one pair on the next card (2 outs) **23/1 (4.3%)**
A flush from a four-flush on the next card (9 outs) **4.2/1 (19%)**
A straight from an open-ended draw on the next card (8 outs) **4.9/1 (17%)**
A straight from a gutshot draw on the next card (4 outs) **11/1 (9%)**
A pair from two non-pair cards (overcards) on the next card (6 outs) **6.8/1 (13%)**
A second pair with your kicker on the next card, when you hold the same pair as your opponent but are 'outkicked' (3 outs) **15/1 (6%)**

From Flop to River

The probability of improving to:

A full house or better from a set by the river **2/1 (33%)**
A full house or better from two pair by the river (4 outs) **5.1/1 (17%)**
A set or better from one pair by the river (2 outs) **11/1 (8.4%)**
A flush from a four-flush by the river (9 outs) **1.9/1 (35%)**
A flush from a three-flush by the river **23/1 (4.2%)**
A straight from an open-ended draw by the river (8 outs) **2.2/1 (32%)**

A straight from a gutshot straight draw by the river (4 outs) **5.1/1 (17%)**

A pair or better from two non-pair cards by the river (6 outs) **3.2/1 (24%)**

A second pair with your kicker by the river, when you hold the same pair as your opponent but are 'outkicked' (3 outs) **7/1 (13%)**

From Turn to River

The probability of improving to:

A full house or better from a set on the final card (10 outs) **3.6/1 (22%)**

A full house from two pair on the final card (4 outs) **11/1 (9%)**

A set from one pair on the final card (2 outs) **22/1 (4.4%)**

A flush from a four-flush on the final card (9 outs) **4.1/1 (20%)**

A straight from an open-ended draw on the final card (8 outs) **4.8/1 (17%)**

A straight from a gutshot draw on the final card (4 outs) **11/1 (9%)**

A pair from two non-pair cards (overcards) on the final card (6 outs) **6.7/1 (13%)**

A second pair with your kicker on the final card, when you hold the same pair as your opponent but are 'outkicked' (3 outs) **14/1 (7%)**

♣ — ♥ — ♦ — ♠ — ♣ — ♥ — ♦ — ♠

Before the Flop Match-Ups (Expected Value)

Pair vs. Pair

A♦-A♥ vs. K♣-K♠ **81.3%-18.7%**

A♦-A♥ vs. 6♣-6♠ **79.8%-20.2%**

Pocket Rockets vs. Big Slick

A♦-A♥ vs. A♣-K♠ **92.6%-7.4%**

A♦-A♥ vs. A♣-K♣ **87.9%-12.1%**

Pocket Rockets vs. Connectors

A♦-A♥ vs. J♣-T♠ **82.0%-18.0%**

A♦-A♥ vs. J♣-T♣ **78.3%-21.7%**

A♦-A♥ vs. 6♣-5♠ **80.6%-19.4%**

A♦-A♥ vs. 6♣-5♣ **76.9%-23.1%**

Pair vs. Two Overcards

T♦-T♥ vs. A♣-K♠ **57.3%-42.7%**
T♦-T♥ vs. A♣-K♣ **53.9%-46.1%**
6♦-6♥ vs. A♣-K♠ **55.4%-44.6%**
6♦-6♥ vs. A♣-K♣ **52.1%-47.9%**
J♦-T♦ vs. 2♣-2♠ **54.0%-46.0%**
J♦-T♥ vs. 2♣-2♠ **51.2%-48.8%**

Pair vs. One Overcard (dominated hand)

K♦-K♥ vs. A♣-K♠ **70.0%-30.0%**
K♦-K♥ vs. A♣-K♣ **65.9%-34.1%**
6♦-6♥ vs. 7♣-6♠ **64.2%-35.8%**
6♦-6♥ vs. 7♣-6♣ **60.5%-39.5%**

Pair vs. One Overcard

K♦-K♥ vs. A♣-Q♠ **71.6%-28.4%**
K♦-K♥ vs. A♣-Q♣ **67.9%-32.1%**
T♦-T♥ vs. Λ♣-2♠ **71.1%-28.9%**
T♦-T♥ vs. A♣-2♣ **67.4%-32.6%**
6♦-6♥ vs. A♣-2♠ **69.9%-30.1%**
6♦-6♥ vs. A♣-2♣ **66.2%-33.8%**

Dominated Hands

A♦-K♥ vs. A♣-Q♠ **74.0%-26.0%**
A♦-K♥ vs. A♣-Q♣ **69.7%-30.3%**
A♦-K♥ vs. A♣-6♠ **73.5%-26.5%**
A♦-K♥ vs. A♣-6♣ **69.2%-30.8%**
A♦-K♥ vs. K♣-Q♠ **74.2%-25.8%**
A♦-K♥ vs. K♣-Q♣ **69.9%-30.1%**
A♦-K♥ vs. K♣-7♠ **75.0%-25.0%**
A♦-K♥ vs. K♣-7♣ **70.7%-29.3%**

Two Overcards vs. Non-Pair

A♦-K♥ vs. 7♣-6♠ **61.5%-38.5%**
A♦-K♥ vs. 7♣-6♣ **57.7%-42.3%**

One Overcard vs. Non-Pair

A♦-2♥ vs. 7♣-6♠ **53.9%-46.1%**

A♦-2♥ vs. 7♣-6♣ **50.4%-49.6%**

Useful Hold'em Odds Resources

http://www.twodimes.net/poker/

http://www.math.sfu.ca/~alspach/pokerdigest.html

Glossary

♣ — ♥ — ♦ — ♠ — ♣ — ♥ — ♦ — ♠

This glossary does not feature every single term which arises in limit hold'em. I will assume that the reader is familiar with extremely obvious terms such as 'bet', 'call', 'turn', 'river', 'flush', 'straight' etc. The following are all in common use in hold'em literature.

Aggressive
A style of play that involves betting and raising rather than checking and calling (see page 12).

All-in
A player who is in a pot but has no more money to bet, or to call bets, is 'all-in'.

Backdoor
To make a hand (usually a flush or straight) by using both the turn and river cards.

Bad beat
A pot that is lost very much against the odds.

Bankroll
The money you have available to play poker.

Blank
A card which arrives on the turn or river and is of no help to anyone.

Board
The cards showing on the table.

Button
The dealer and the player to speak last on all post-flop rounds.

Call cold
To call two or more bets without having already invested money on a particular betting round.

Call down
To play a heads-up situation by simply calling all bets by the opponent with the aim of reaching a showdown.

Cap
To make the third raise on a betting round after which no further raising – on that round – is possible.

Check-raise
To check and then raise when the opponent bets.

Connectors
Cards of adjacent rank, e.g. 6-5, K-Q.

Counterfeit
When a card appears that kills all or part of your holding. For example, the board is A-J-9-3 and you hold A-3 and have two pair. If the river is a jack your second pair is counterfeit and is thus worthless.

Crying call
To call on the river without any great hope of your hand being good, usually when you have just been outdrawn.

Cut-off
The position before the button.

Dominated (hand)
A dominated hand is one where an 'improving' card doesn't help as it also makes the opponent's hand stronger. For example, A-K dominates K-J as hitting a king does not help the latter hand.

Double belly-buster
A double gutshot draw, for example J-10 with a board of A-Q-8 when either a king or 9 will complete a straight.

Draw, drawing hand
A hand that has a reasonable chance to improve, usually to a straight or a flush.

Early position
The first three players to speak, pre-flop, in a full ring game of ten players.

Fish
A weak player, usually playing in a loose/passive style.

Fold
To throw away one's hand.

Free card
To receive a card without having had to invest money in the pot.

Freeroll
To be splitting the pot but with a chance to improve to a winning hand. For example, if you have K♠-Q♠ and your opponent has K♥-Q♣ with a board of A♠-J♦-10♠. You both hold the top straight and it is impossible for you to lose the pot. However, you have a chance (with any spade) to improve to a flush and thus win.

Full ring game
A game with all 10 players at the table.

Get away (from a hand)
To fold a decent, but worse, hand and avoid losing extra bets.

Getting (giving) heat
When pressure is applied with bets and raises.

Gutshot
A draw to a straight relying on just one card, e.g. 6-5 with a board of 8-9-K is hoping for a 7 to complete the straight (see also *open-ended*).

Hand history
The details of the hand that has just been played. This only applies to online play. A key feature of this is that (on most sites) it is possible to see what a player was holding if they lost a showdown on the river. In live play a losing player rarely has to reveal their hand in this way.

Handle
The name (usually pseudonym) used by an online player.

Heads-up
A pot contested between two players.

Implied odds
The odds you can expect from a pot due to potential future action.

Junk
A worthless hand.

Kicker
The sidecard to the main hand. For example, you hold A-K and an opponent A-J. The board is A-9-8-4-2. You both have a pair of aces but you win with your sidecard: your king kicker beating his jack kicker.

Late blind
A player who joins a game has the option of posting a 'late blind' (in any non-blind seat other than the button) rather than waiting for the big blind to come round to them. This is usually done from the cut-off seat.

Late position
The cut-off and button seats.

Lead out
To be first to speak and bet on any post-flop betting round.

Limp
To call the big blind pre-flop rather than raising.

Loose
To play too many hands (see page 11).

Maniac
A player who bets and raises much more than is justified by their holdings.

Middle position
The seats between early position and late position, typically the 4th, 5th and 6th seats after the blinds in a ten-player ring game.

Muck
To throw away your hand.

Nut(s)
A currently unbeatable hand. Also used are nut straight and nut flush for the best hand in those categories.

Offsuit
Cards of differing suits.

On tilt
To play recklessly, usually after suffering unfortunate losses.

Open-ended
A draw to a straight where there are two possible cards to complete the draw, e.g. 10-9 with a board of J-8-2. Here either a queen or a 7 will complete the straight (see also *gutshot*).

Outdraw
To receive a card which improves your hand, so that you now are beating your opponent.

-outer (e.g. four-outer)
A hand which has a precise number of outs, e.g. a gutshot draw – requiring a card of a certain rank – is a four-outer.

Outkick
To beat an opponent who holds the same hand as you thanks to a better sidecard (see also *kicker*).

Outs
Cards which will improve your hand – possibly turning it into a winner.

Overcard(s)
Card(s) ranking higher than any of the board cards.

Overpair
A pair ranking higher than any of the board cards.

Passive
A style of play relying on checking and calling rather than betting and raising (see page 12).

Pay-off hand
A hand which is too good to fold but is nevertheless second best, and thus results in you 'paying off' your opponent.

(to) Play back
To suddenly become the aggressor having previously been passive in the pot.

Position
Your seat at the table relative to your opponent(s).

Pot odds
The size of the pot relative to the size of the bet you are facing. Pot odds are used to calculate whether calling a bet represents good value.

Protect(ing) a hand
Betting or raising with a good, but vulnerable, holding.

Quads
Four of a kind.

Rags
Low cards that most likely do not connect with players' hands.

Rainbow
A flop which features three different suits (so that a flush draw is not possible) is a rainbow flop.

Rake
The percentage of the pot taken by the house (or online site). Online this is typically $1-$3 per pot.

Read
To figure out (correctly or otherwise) what cards the opponents hold.

Redraw
The turn card improves an opponent's holding such that they now have the best hand. You then improve on the river to beat them.

Reload
To bring more money to the table after you have lost your stack.

Represent
To suggest a certain holding by your betting and/or raising.

Re-raise
To raise in response to a raise.

Rock
A very tight player.

Rockets
Aces.

Runner-runner
To make a hand by receiving helpful cards on both the turn and the river.

Semi-bluff
To bluff when you also have some chance to improve to the best hand.

Set
Three of a kind made by having a pair in your hand which matches a board card.

Short-handed
A game featuring few players, typically five or less.

Short-stacked
To run short of money on the table, so that you may find yourself 'all-in' at some point during a pot.

Showdown
When the cards are revealed at the end of the hand.

Side pot
A side pot is created when one player is 'all-in' and has no further funds to bet or call bets. The all-in player competes only for the main pot, and the other players in the hand compete for both the main pot and the side pot.

Slowplay
To bet timidly – checking and/or calling – to represent weakness when actually holding a strong hand.

Stack
The money you have available on the table.

Steal
To win the pot without any hand at all simply by betting and everyone else folding.

Steaming
To play over-aggressively, usually after losing a big pot.

Strong
A style of play which is typically tight/aggressive (see page 14).

Tainted outs
Cards that improve your hand, but unfortunately give an opponent an even stronger hand.

Tight
A style of play whereby a player plays very few hands (see page 11)

Trap hand
A hand which, by its nature, causes you to lose money.

Trash
A worthless hand.

Trips
Three of a kind made by having a card in your hand which matches a pair on the board.

Under-the-gun (UTG)
The player first to speak in the pre-flop betting round.

Weak
A style of play which is typically loose/passive (see page 14).

Whiplash
To be whiplashed is to call a bet or raise and then face a further raise (or raises) on the same betting round.

Further Reading

♣ — ♥ — ♦ — ♠ — ♣ — ♥ — ♦ — ♠

Recommended Titles

The following books all have excellent material relating to playing hold'em at the middle limits. *Small Stakes Hold'em* is aimed primarily at beating games below the $15-$30 level, but has much advice which will be useful when you run into weak players at any limit. *Killer Poker Online* does not deal with any specific playing strategies, but has so much excellent advice about online poker in general that it cannot fail to help you to improve your game.

Hold'em Poker for Advanced Players (21st Century edition), Mason Malmuth and David Sklansky (Two Plus Two Publishing 1999)

Internet Texas Hold'em, Matthew Hilger (Matthew Hilger 2003)

Killer Poker Online, John Vorhaus (Lyle Stuart 2003)

Middle Limit Hold'em Poker, Bob Ciaffone and Jim Brier (Bob Ciaffone 2002)

Small Stakes Hold'em, Ed Miller, David Sklansky (Two Plus Two Publishing 2004)